I0095898

DISSOCIATION IN LATE MODERN AMERICA

A DEFENSE AGAINST SOUL?

LAURA K KERR, PHD

K

LK KERR
BOOKS

Copyright © 2010, 2014, 2022 by Laura K Kerr, PhD

All rights reserved.

No part of this book may be reproduced in any form or by any electronic or
mechanical means, including information storage and retrieval systems,
without written permission from the author, except for the use of brief
quotations in a book review, article, or scholarly work.

Trade paperback ISBN: 979-8-9857460-2-0

Ebook ISBN: 978-0-615-97731-7

Edited by Jefferson, FirstEditing

∾

LK Kerr Books
laurakkerrr.com
PO Box 27152, San Francisco CA 94127-0152

CONTENTS

For Gus,
for making me one of the lucky ones.
&

In memory of
Len Dan "Danny" Kerr III
1962–2008

ABSTRACT

Dissociation typically describes a psychological defense that protects the psyche from emotionally overwhelming events. However, dissociation can also contribute to maintaining and restoring relationships after suffering traumatic stress and overwhelming social strain. Two aspects of late modern American society interfere with dissociation's contribution to social change: 1) the Enlightenment conception of human nature, on which American democracy is based, and 2) America's sharp distinctions between public and private spheres of life. Using research on human evolution, neuroscience, trauma, and Jungian psychology, *Dissociation in Late Modern America* shows how Americans have become dependent on dissociative defenses in everyday life, challenging their capacity for soulful connections and living.

1

TRAUMA NATION

The situation which I believe we are all facing in the world today was one which the primitive world, the past life of Africa, knew only too well. It is a loss of the first spirit, or to put it in the old-fashioned way, a loss of soul. Before my day with the Zulu prophet was over, I knew that he regarded this as the greatest calamity that could come to human beings.

—Laurens van der Post, *The Heart of the Hunter*

The English language lacks a word to describe the emotional suffering caused by human cruelty. Words exist for damaging actions—*abuse, rape, assault*—but the aftereffects are devoid of such singular representation. Medicine attempts to remedy the problem by introducing the word *trauma* into our common vocabulary. The *Oxford English Dictionary* defines *trauma* as an external bodily injury and the condition that emerges in its aftermath (1989). When William James used the term in 1895 to relay the psychological impact of mentally unbearable events, he described it as "thorns in the spirit" (as cited in *Oxford*

English Dictionary, 1989). For those whose lives are irrevocably altered by cruelty, there may be no better description.

Yet *trauma* is the word we inherited. In part, this is due to the powerful analogies that can be made between physical and psychological suffering. Just as a knife wound forever leaves a scar, our relationships can irrevocably alter us. *Trauma* attests to the biological component of psychological pain, which not only leaves its imprint on the brain but also extends beyond it, registering somatically throughout the body. Even when people "forget" trauma, it continues to have an impact through conditions as varied as obesity, depression, ischemic heart disease, and cancer (Felitti et al., 1998).

The term *trauma* also provides a way to speak generally about radically disparate situations with universal characteristics. Whether a person is a soldier in war, a displaced survivor of climate catastrophe, someone who has endured chronic family violence, or the victim of an assault or rape, responses to such travesties transcend the particulars of both situation and personal suffering. Nightmares, hyperarousal, and dissociation become signs of "thorns in the spirit," piercing the psyches of those who have been pushed beyond their mental breaking point (Herman, 1997). By describing these responses as *traumatic*, we witness the universal impact of cruelty to which all are vulnerable.

The success of the term *trauma,* as well as *dissociation* and other words used to describe psychological defenses protecting the psyche from traumatic events, is likely due to the prominent role medicine plays in many Westerners' lives. Medicine leaves few human experiences unexplained or uncontrolled. Sleep, sex, relationships, diet—how we behave, feel, and think —can be meticulously described and regulated through medicine. This includes the hurt we inflict on one another.

The field of medicine has made some of the most profound, social-altering contributions to modern society. During the past

50 years, due to rapid advances in microbiology, many people who once may have died prematurely or survived but with grave disability can now live productively, although often with chronic illnesses to manage. This development has irrevocably changed attitudes towards many diseases and engendered the belief that if we delve deeply enough into the secrets of human genes and other microscopic aspects of our bodies, we can escape many afflictions and much suffering.

Not surprisingly, in medicine many find a remedy and philosophy for what it means to be human. Particularly in the West, many are increasingly fixated on the body as the source of suffering and where healing occurs. Many of us are also uncomfortable with distinctions between what is right and wrong in our relativistic society, preferring instead to discriminate between what is normal or abnormal, identifying what is "healthy" in ourselves and others, in effect treating life as the pursuit of chronic health as much as the avoidance of death and chronic disease (Kerr, 2007). Yet medical models, when they become the primary arbiters of the human condition, can inadvertently silence sources of suffering that cannot be found in the human body. Furthermore, what cannot be represented through the lens of medicine and scientific rationality is often debased as pathology.

Dissociation is a case in point. As Jungian analyst James Hillman observed, "The phenomena of dissociation—breaking away, splitting off, personification, multiplication, ambivalence—will always seem an illness to the ego as it has come to be defined" (1975, p. 25). Here Hillman points to identification with the ego and conscious awareness, characteristic of scientific thought and modern thinking. From the vantage of the ego, there is no soul, no spirit, and certainly no "thorns in the spirit." What is real can be measured and often controlled. In some ways, medicalizing the aftereffects of cruelty is a humane course of action, even if this means the person suffering becomes pathologized. Otherwise, they risk being ignored.

In this monograph, which began as a master's thesis for my counseling degree in depth psychology at Pacifica Graduate Institute, I attempt to step outside the shadow of the medical model and the rationalistic, ego-driven perspective used to address the aftereffects of human cruelty. I believe both devalue the rich emotional life that enlivens our imaginal worlds and gives breath to our souls. Humans are much more than rational beings. We are also deeply emotional and sustained by social bonds created through emotional connections. As Carl G. Jung once remarked, "The essential basis of our personality is affectivity. Thought and action are, as it were, only symptoms of affectivity" (as cited in Kalsched, 1996, p. 88).

I share research from neuroscience, anthropology, psychology, primatology, sociology, and evolutionary theory that chronicle how human survival has depended on the development of an extensive emotional repertoire, enabling us to communicate and become attached to others and find meaning and purpose through relationships. From the perspective of this emerging body of research, rather than referring to modern humans as *Homo sapiens sapiens*—meaning "wise man"—a better moniker might be *Homo emotional,* which, according to the etymology of *emotion,* would mean those who move out of themselves, migrating towards others in search of human connection (*Oxford English Dictionary,* 1989). Such a change would respect the necessity of emotions and human relationships for our survival as a species. It would also bring us closer to witnessing the loss of soul in our late modern American society.

Hillman defined the soul as "a functional complex of the psyche, acting as a mediating personality between the whole psyche, which is mainly unconscious" (1972, p. 51). I believe this mediating quality of soul arises from the deeply relational nature of human beings. As Thomas Moore observed, intimacy is a sign of the presence of soul. "When the soul is alive in us we can make connections, be involved, and feel in touch with the people around us and the things we do" (2008, p. 31). Through emotional connections we emerge with soul and the ability to connect with *anima mundi*, the soulful spirit animating and connecting all matter and life. Hillman made a similar point:

> Not a diamond but a sponge, not a private flame but a flowing participation, a knotted complexity of strands whose entanglements are also "yours" and "theirs." The collective nature of the soul's depths means simply that no man is an island. (p. 24)

In contrast, the current emphasis on wisdom in the characterization of the human species likely says more about Western civilization than the nature of humanity. The designation *Homo sapiens* emerged with Enlightenment attitudes that stressed the power of rational thought over emotions. Since the Enlightenment, emotions have characteristically been associated with "primitive" societies, the feminine, the mentally ill, and animals.

Though Enlightenment ideals persist and are reflected by the prominence of the medical model, we have also entered a new era of modern society, what sociologist Ulrich Beck (1999) described as *risk society* and *second modernity* and which I will refer to as *late modern society*. Late modern society is in part distinguished by its members' inability to believe that rational thought will lead to human progress as the architects of the Enlightenment once hoped. On the contrary, late moderns must contend with the fallout of the Enlightenment project. In late modernity, Beck and colleagues argued, "The future becomes the unforeseeable, the accidental, that which cannot be planned for, that which cannot be controlled"—a sharp distinction from the Enlightenment's scientifically driven emphasis on prediction and control (2003, p. 10). According to sociologist Anthony Giddens, the outcome is an experimental and traumatizing state of affairs:

> It is not an experiment in the laboratory sense, because we do not govern the outcome within fixed parameters—it is more like a dangerous adventure, in which each of us has to participate whether we like it or not. (1994, p. 59)

Many Americans feel the effects of trauma in their personal lives. Ample evidence suggests the American home has become an emotionally damaging environment (Anda et al., 2004; Whitfield, 2004). Childhood abuse, neglect, and other emotionally damaging experiences—such as witnessing domestic violence or living with a substance abuser—are so prevalent that trauma specialist and psychiatrist Bessel van der Kolk claimed adverse childhood experiences are the single most important health problem facing Americans today (2008). Extensive research shows adverse childhood experiences are linked with most mental disorders, increased suicide attempts, and alcohol, drug, and nicotine abuse (Chapmana et al., 2004; Dube et al., 2001; Edwards et al., 2003). Furthermore, psychologist Patricia Tomich of Kent State University, who looked at the role of traumatic events in college students' lives, observed greater distress when the traumatic event was intentional, such as an assault, than when it was unintentional, such as a natural disaster or death of a loved one (2007).

While early modernity associated silencing emotions with advancing society, today not feeling has become a necessary defense against both personal wounds and a traumatized—and traumatizing—world. In this monograph, I look at dissociation as a defense against feeling the emotional impact of personal trauma and as a symptom of the failure of the Enlightenment project and the conception of humanity on which it is based.

My arguments are a response to the conditions in late modern America and its sharp distinction between public and private life and emphasis on protecting individual freedoms at the expense of the collective—which the medical model implicitly defends when it identifies pathology in the body irrespective of the origins of suffering. I will discuss dissociation as a sign of suffering that points to the loss of the social-emotional bonds that are fundamental to our human experience and necessary for much-needed social transformation. This project is not an attempt to debase rationality; instead, I am highlighting the centrality of emotions and the soul for our individual and collective well-being.

The medical model is not the focus of this project, although I believe it is one of American society's primary methods for silencing the wounding resulting from our collective failure to honor our need for social-emotional bonds. Like many Americans, the medical model has played a central role in my own narrative and efforts to overcome the thorns in my spirit. Nearly two decades ago, I was diagnosed with a mental disorder that I was told would require lifelong treatment with medications. For a while the drugs "worked" in the sense that they allowed me to function within the constraints of late modern American society, but I also experienced deep feelings of grief and loss. I often felt disconnected from others, yet I lacked the courage to address the parts of myself that restrained me from connecting in meaningful ways. Like too many people, my childhood was marred by abuse and neglect, which limited my capacity for intimacy. It wasn't until I had the courage to address my wounds that I could fully appreciate the love in my life, trust love, and trust myself. After much psychotherapy and soul-searching, and with the support of caring and loving people, I was able to eventually end my dependency on medications and build a meaningful life with others and with soul.

Interpreting my symptoms as traumatic responses to my

childhood conditions was central to my return to growth and meaningfully connecting with others. It gave me an origin story, returning me to my first family as the source of my suffering, which opposed the genetic model of mental illness my psychiatrists impressed upon me and used to justify treating my suffering with medications. Whereas my origin story felt more accurate, it also pointed to my parents' victimization as children, and hence, the intergenerational nature of childhood abuse and family violence.

Eventually, I began identifying connections between family violence, childhood abuse, and the emotionally corrosive conditions of modern living. This led to my search for ways to recover from trauma in all its forms, which I believe requires returning social-emotional bonds and the soul to their rightful place as central aspects of human experience. This has also meant finding an alternative to the medical model's understanding of what it means to be human.

The "Pharmacracy" as Area of Interest

Some argue medicine, and psychiatry in particular, should have no role in treating trauma. By locating trauma in the body, medicine implicitly severs connections between human suffering and the inhumane conditions that cause traumatic reactions (Burstow, 2003; Wilkerson, 1998). Nevertheless, biological changes occur when a person is a victim of interpersonal trauma, as human cruelty is often called. However, my greatest concern is that awareness of the impact of trauma has failed to stop its occurrence like a vaccination halts the spread of a virus. Instead, while our awareness of the properties and treatment of interpersonal trauma has increased over the past century, savagery against women and children, wars, genocide, and other manners of violence have also increased, and there seems no limit to the human imagination for ways to inflict cruelty. With medicine—particularly biomedical psychiatry—as the primary method for treating psychological trauma, opportunities to find alternative ways to impede thorns from entering spirits in the first place have not been forthcoming.

The reason for medicine's continued role in treating trauma, despite its failure to halt conditions that lead to trauma in the first place, could be that it enforces a particular sense of responsibility, and hence, a particular form of society. As several leading trauma psychiatrists have observed, "The issue of responsibility, both individual and shared, is at the very core of how a society defines itself" (van der Kolk et al., 1996, p. xi).

The psychiatrist Thomas Szasz went so far as to argue that medicine's prominence is a major reason for the decline of democracy in American society (2001). Szasz claimed we have become a *pharmacracy*, a society governed by medicine's understanding of humanity in which "people perceive all manner of human problems as medical in nature, susceptible to medical remedies" (p. xvi). As medicine became a dominant arbiter of truths about and solutions for the human condition, values were also transformed. Szasz proposed that an ethic has emerged supporting accountability for our good deeds while excusing our bad deeds (and less than desirable traits), depicting the latter as the result of diseases and disorders. The outcome is a nation of people who evade responsibility for their actions, blaming diseases and genetic inheritance for behaviors that at one time would have reflected poor character or irresponsibility. In effect, medicine undermines personal responsibility, and consequently, the very fabric of society.

Medicine's influence on how we perceive ourselves and the solutions we create to address our problems is hard to ignore. Many behaviors once deemed sinful—such as drug abuse, mental disorders, suicide, and even violence—are often related to traumas unhealed or denied, and through the medical model, they are recast as pathologies of the body or genetics and thus conceived as at least partially outside individual responsibility. This has its advantages. The dominant genetic-based understanding of mental disorders validates the belief that compassion and assistance are needed for overcoming our limitations, so it often opposes the judgment and alienation that sometimes meet the most troubled members of society. The philosopher and historian of science Georges Canguilhem wrote:

> Through genetics the sick person is no longer a "bad boy," but instead is like a "poor land" that is bad due not to moral fault but to physical constitution: "disease is no longer related to individual responsibility; no more imprudence, no more excess to incriminate. . . . . As sick men we are the effect of universal mixing, love, and chance. (1966/1991, p. 278)

A cursory glance at the events leading to the creation of the United States of America reveals an underlying reason why a genetic-based understanding of human nature and the medical model are so appealing in this country today. From its inception, American democracy was designed to balance the rights of citizens with their societal responsibilities. Through this balance a commonwealth would be created that benefited all members of society. The attention to personal rights reflected the conditions of the people whose exodus from their home countries led to the creation of the United States. Many had escaped religious persecution and other forms of oppression in their homelands. Though they came from many different societies and held many different beliefs, they shared the traumatizing effects common to all people with histories of oppression and persecution.

The formation of American democracy and law may be inseparable from the trauma many experienced. Avoiding the repetition of past traumas led to a new understanding of what it meant to be human, one that protected against threats to religious freedom and elevated individual rights above social responsibilities. As philosopher Martha Nussbaum (2006) observed, in America human consciousness became depicted as a self-directed yet fragile space that must be protected from the impingement of social forces. This understanding of what it meant to be human was based on Enlightenment ideals that upheld human qualities such as rational choice, free will, intentionality, and agency. This emerging sense of humanity was also a subtle and convenient defense against the deep emotional wounding that drove many people to America in the first place. As Giddens remarked, "The emotional life of modern civilization was essentially written out of Enlightenment philosophy," which was done to escape societies perceived as tightly bound by tradition (1994, p. 68).

Through democracy and the image of humankind as rational beings, the yokes of orthodoxy and aristocracy were thrown off, and the belief that all humans were created equal through the faculty of human reason began to hold sway. Granted, in the beginning only men of European descent benefited from this, but a blueprint for equality was set for future efforts to recognize the free will of all citizens, irrespective of gender, race, disability, or any other difference.

Today genes challenge reason for the role of the great equalizer. Instead of the principle of universal, inalienable rights uniting us, many are increasingly bound to the belief that deep down all are made of the same stuff—genes—and it is our common biology that makes us equal. Genes can be much more equitable than the notion of human reason ever was. Unlike reason, genes have always been identified as belonging to everyone, not just men of European descent. And while genetics has been used to oppress—eugenics is a cautionary reminder of how easily science can be exploited to nefarious ends—it has also undermined notions about superior races and inferior bodies by revealing our shared traits and vulnerabilities. In this gene-based form of democracy, Szasz (2001) seems at least partially correct: medicine has become a common hope for salvation from disorders and diseases that might otherwise limit social standing and opportunities for equal access to resources and achievement.

Szasz (2001) is also correct that responsibility is a problem in our emerging pharmacracy, but rather than our sense of personal responsibility being undermined by a proliferation of diseases for every human condition, it is the absence of shared responsibility that most threatens democratic ideals. The American notion of democracy may not have intended the idea of rights without responsibility, but it has become an undeniable outcome. It is in this social context that the terms *trauma* and *genetics* have taken root, rapidly growing in our common vernacular and becoming socially acceptable, no-fault ways of talking about the scars left by emotionally damaging human encounters without requiring changes in the conditions perpetuating the need for such discourse.

Despite the appeal of the genetic story of human origins, evidence reveals the social environment plays as much, if not more, of an influence on the kinds of people we become (Jablonka & Lamb, 2005). Particularly in psychiatry, the genetic explanation for what it means to be human seems more wishful thinking than science when used to identify the origin of mental disorders. For example, studies that claimed a serotonin transporter gene (5-*HTTLPR*) is responsible for the development of depression were shown through a meta-analysis to be patently false (Risch et al., 2009). Furthermore, despite claims that schizophrenia is likely a genetic disorder, seven out of ten instances of schizophrenia arise without any family history of the disorder (Maxmen et al., 2009, p. 305). In fact, after decades of research, no correlations have been found between specific genes and mental disorders, which the

Mendelian model of genetics demands. According to psychiatrist Kenneth Kendler:

> For psychiatric disorders, individual genes appear to have a quite modest association with psychiatric illness. While they may have an impact on risk, individual genes hardly predetermine illness, as would be expected if we had discovered "genes for" mental disorders. (2005, p. 1247)

The practice of treating mental disorders with medications is theoretically supported by the belief that genetic inheritance is the fundamental mechanism for their transmission. Certainly, a biologically based approach to treatment would make sense if the origins of mental disorders are genes, the fundamental building blocks of the human body. However, not only is there insufficient evidence to support this conclusion, but the medications have failed to lead to health. For example, one review article revealed the duplicity surrounding published accounts of the efficacy of selective serotonin reuptake inhibitors, or SSRI antidepressants (Turner et al., 2008). The article concluded that pharmaceutical companies and psychiatric researchers mainly published studies confirming the effectiveness of SSRI antidepressants, generally excluding studies that had negative or questionable results. The review showed there has been an overstatement of the efficacy of these antidepressants by as much as 30 percent.

Some of the most damning evidence against the medical model of mental disorders comes from investigative reporter Robert Whitaker. After combing through decades of psychiatric research, Whitaker concluded that the current practice of treating mental illnesses as chronic disorders requiring continuous medication is a "failed paradigm of care" (Hall, 2009). According to Whitaker, psychopharmacology is actually *creating* chronic illness. He observed that since the arrival of

Thorazine and Haloperidol, which marked the beginning of the widespread treatment of mental illness with medications over 50 years ago, patient outcomes have been getting worse. More people have become disabled by mental illness. They suffer from more physical ailments, are more chronically ill, are straddled with higher unemployment, and are dying as much as 25 years younger on average. Furthermore, evidence suggests that medications perturb otherwise normal functioning—including normal mental functioning.

Genes certainly play a role in the development of mental disorders (and humankind), but how they do, and to what extent, remains unknown. However, ample evidence supports the conclusion that stressful and traumatic life events are highly correlated with the development of mental disorders (Whitfield, 2004). Indeed, Risch and colleagues reached a similar conclusion about depression, stating, "Stressful life events have a potent relationship with the risk of depression" (2009, p. 2468).

While theory failure is a natural event in the progression of any science, the probable demise of the genetic theory of mental disorders does not follow the course of normal scientific inquiry. Despite the lack of substantiated evidence, the theory has been treated as a proven fact. As the researchers conducting a meta-analysis of serotonin gene studies concluded, the biggest problem may not be the failure to provide genetic evidence. Instead, "the findings of . . . nonreplicated genetic associations are now being translated to a range of clinical, legal, research, and social settings such as forensics, diagnostic testing, study participants, and the general public" (Risch et al., 2009, p. 2469).

That so many have become attached to the genetic story of mental disorders leads me to believe that there is much that cannot be said about why we suffer. As Michel Foucault observed, "Silence itself . . . is less the absolute limit of discourse . . . than an element that functions alongside the things said" (1984/1990, p. 27). I believe that what has been silenced is our collective need for a deeper, more meaningful sense of community, which has become anemic in current American society as a result of the cavernous division between the public and private spheres of life and America's emphasis on protecting individual rights at the expense of communal needs. I am not arguing there is anything wrong with protecting individual rights. Rather, I am challenging the idea that human nature is determined more by nature (genes) than nurture (social environment), proposed by the medical model of mental disorders.

Looking for the contours of the silences that support the emerging pharmacracy involves asking why so much money, time, and energy is spent developing the genetic theory of mental disorders—and devoting copious funding for developing psychotropic medications—when environmental stressors and human cruelty are already rigorously associated with mental disorders and emotional suffering. I believe I have found one of the answers: we fail to sufficiently mobilize against human cruelty because we have come to rely on medicine to silence the thorns in our spirits. Through psychotropic medications, feelings are numbed. Through the genetic model of human nature, our collective responsibility to relieve human suffering is ignored. In the end the situations that led to suffering in the first place fail to change—although the elevation of individual rights over collective emotional needs remains.

In many regards, interpreting the aftereffects of human cruelty through the medical model is similar to how survivors of chronic abuse avoid reminders of traumatic events and the intense emotions stirred when unconscious memories are triggered. Those who study trauma's effects describe this fragile forgetting as *dissociation*: the human capacity to wall off emotions and memories connected to traumatic events, separating them from conscious awareness (Steinberg & Schnall, 2000). But dissociation is not limited to individual minds. As trauma specialist Judith Herman pointed out, "Repression, dissociation and denial are phenomena of social as well as individual consciousness" (1997, p. 9).

Today both individuals and the collective American society show signs of dissociative defenses, signaling traumatic pasts. Concerning individuals, dissociative defenses become pathological when they are no longer needed to ward off the threats of a traumatizing environment or event (Herman, 1997). Similarly, the conditions of late modern society reveal a pathological continuation of an early defense system that emerged with the split of the modern world from traditional forms of social organization, elevating rational thought while debasing emotional needs. Furthermore, not only does our peculiar form of democracy no longer serve us, but it may also eventually lead to our demise. If the current form of American democracy continues to be exported across the world, with its particular association of individual rights with commodity-driven individualism, the result may be not only the destruction of the planet but also the end of democracy.

Granted, we have medicine to thank for bringing attention to the long-term impact of human cruelty on our psyches. The psychiatrist Charles Samuel Myers coined the term *shellshock*, which recognized that the very nature of war psychologically damaged men exposed to its brutal conditions (van der Kolk et al., 1996, p. 48). Furthermore, it took defining *child abuse* as a medical category in 1965 for a nationwide movement to take hold devoted to protecting children (Hacking, 1991). To be sure, without medicine, we would not only have failed to identify how cruelty harms psyches, but we would also lack methods for healing the wounds left in its wake. Yet with each discovery of the impact of trauma, a counterforce has guaranteed its erasure. Trauma theorist Bessel A. van der Kolk and colleagues witnessed how this erasure mimics the way individuals forget traumatic experiences: "Mirroring the intrusions, confusion, and disbelief of victims whose lives are suddenly shattered by traumatic experiences, the psychiatric profession has gone through periods of fascination with trauma, followed by periods of stubborn disbelief about the relevance of patients' stories" (1996, p. 47).

Remaining aware of trauma requires a different understanding of human nature than the one proposed by the medical model—one that includes all contributing factors to trauma and mental disorders. Ending human cruelty requires empathy for suffering, yet empathy is minimized or lost when dissociative defenses predominate. New methodologies are needed that can go beyond purely rational perspectives and argumentation that perpetuate ego consciousness and ignore intuitive and emotional ways of knowing. In the next section, I introduce alchemical hermeneutics as a method to create a soulful approach to researching. Such an approach helps uncover what is categorically lost when research is conducted with a rationalistic worldview.

Alchemical Hermeneutics as Research Methodology

As a scholar, I have devoted much of my life to using research to shape a more humane mental health system. I have been continually struck by the shell game that brings trauma into focus, only to later hide it from view. While I once believed my research contributed to revealing such sleights of hand, I have started to witness how some of my own scholarship unknowingly contributed to silencing trauma's effects.

My dissertation (2000), my first extended piece of scholarship, chronicled how and why people come to understand psychic suffering as evidence of a mental disorder, and hence, a disease. In part, it was organized by Michel Foucault's notion of the *matrix of experience* (Foucault, 1984/1990). The matrix of experience represents what Foucault came to believe were the three most significant contributors to the complex experience of becoming a self in Western societies. Like Foucault, I believe that what constitutes selfhood is at least in part determined by historical, cultural, and social conditions. Unlike Foucault, I do not believe selfhood—and its expression through experiences such as sexuality, mental illness, and disease—is wholly a "historically singular form of experience" (as cited in Rabinow, 1994, p. 199). While the matrix of experience is a useful way of examining how history, culture, and society make possible some ways of becoming a self while disavowing other possibilities, I believe other aspects of human experience are also universal and deeply ingrained.

The matrix of experience is a tripartite of influences, including 1) a *field of knowledge*, such as biomedical psychiatry, and its concepts, theories, and diverse subspecialties; 2) a *collection of rules* governing our choices between what is acceptable and unacceptable, normal and abnormal, good and evil, ordering the options available for self-making; and 3) the *methods of self-relation* available for creating a relationship with oneself that speaks to the kind of person one is in relation to others (Foucault, 1984/1990). For Foucault, at the core of the matrix of experience resided *thought*, the primary characteristic identifying an individual as a knowing and ethical subject and a person who can distinguish between true and false, right and wrong, and refuse or accept rules for herself and others.

According to Foucault, all actions could be reduced to thought. Foucault perceived thought as the most fundamental aspect of the modern experience of selfhood: "There is no experience that is not a way of thinking and cannot be analyzed from the viewpoint of the history of thought" (as cited in Rabinow, 1994, p. 201). This is not a surprising conclusion, given

Foucault's examination of selfhood as a product of the sciences and social norms of Western civilization. For example, in his reflections on sexuality and mental illness as examples of the creation of selfhood, he retained modernity's perception of thought (and reason) as the central, if not elevated, aspect of all human experience.

Missing from such a project are emotions and other deep stirrings, although there are legitimate reasons for their minimization in Foucault's (1984/1990) matrix of experience. His efforts were directed towards uncovering the origins of power and oppression hidden in the universal truths produced by scientific discourses and how these were manipulated in the construction of selfhood. An accurate chronicling could minimize the role of emotions since emotions were often ignored in the construction of modern thought through the exaltation of reason.

Emotions, of course, do exist, and our late modern world is not amenable to analyses that ignore their importance. While analyses such as Foucault's identify how the sense of selfhood is influenced by discourse—of which the genetic story of mental illness is a prime example—they omit the emotions silenced by these discourses, which nevertheless contribute to our experiences of selfhood and the construction of the world we inhabit.

Reconnecting with emotions is vitally needed in our era of planet destruction, in which, as ecophilosopher Derrick Jensen pointed out:

In the last 24 hours, over 200,000 acres of rainforest were destroyed. Thirteen million tons of toxic chemicals were released. Forty-five thousand people died of starvation, thirty-eight thousand of them children. More than one hundred plant or animal species went extinct because of civilized humans. (2006, p. 341)

Such destruction is emotionally unfathomable and emotionally blunting. Only in a society that habitually silences emotions can so many of us carry on, living within the system causing destruction while continually attempting to step outside of it, which, no doubt, is part of modernity—that continual need to destroy in order to create—and contributes to the erasure of trauma left in its wake. But silencing emotions has not lessened the need for mourning our losses. And when a loss cannot be mourned, it changes the very landscape of life.

According to Greg Mogenson, "The mourning of losses and the making of cultures are synonymous activities" (as cited in Romanyshyn, 2007, p. 76). Mogenson's connection between mourning and culture provides insight into America's continual need for creation out of destruction. If Mogenson is correct about the formation of culture, it may be that our collective denial of our need to mourn emerged with the silencing of emotions.

Emotions are a fundamental aspect of all humans, irrespective of culture. Our society's addiction to continual rebirth belies an inner sense of profound loss, if not deadness, that results when how we think is habitually deemed superior to how we feel. America increasingly reminds me of the poet Robert Lowell's experience of depression: "All winter I've had an uncomfortable feeling of dying into rebirth ... the flat prose of coming to an end of one way of life, whittled down and whittled down and picking up nothing new though always about to" (as cited in Goodwin & Jamison, 1990, p. 21). The inability to mourn may be the collective psychological problem of our time and *is* our culture. Without opportunities to mourn, we are doomed to repeat our futile grasping at renewal, which to date has resulted in the continual destruction of the planet and each other.

For many, it is not the destruction of the planet that weighs heaviest on their spirits but the deep wounds of childhood and other traumas. The inability to mourn our wounds leaves many of us too numb to sufficiently mobilize and alter the course of our democracy enough to divert its demise. As old wounds are continually silenced, the original conditions of trauma are recreated, which affects the lives of the people treated clinically, the research methods used, the truths deconstructed, and the new truths created. I see this in my dissertation, in which I created an account of how people learned to interpret their suffering as evidence of a mental disorder while never revealing in words the profound grief I felt with each narrative I relayed —as well as the loss I felt for the story I did not tell, my own. Psychologist Francine Shapiro observed, "Unless the trauma can be incorporated into existing schemata, the information will remain in active memory and will break through in intrusive thoughts. This process alternates with numbing and avoidance until some integration results" (2001, p. 21). My critical Foucauldian stance never led to the integration I yearned for, as I continued to silence my emotions in efforts to become a rational-minded theorist.

Thus, in my own research, I witness my failure to mourn even as my grief informed my choice of scholars quoted, testimonies relayed, and historical influences identified. Thoughts and ideas give only hazy glimpses of grief. Using patient narratives did not dispel this murkiness, because the people I quoted inhabited the same world I did—one that inadvertently silences sources of trauma in the construction of mental disorders according to the medical model of chronic diseases.

The language of symptoms often takes precedence over the language of mourning in clinical encounters, yet anyone who has lost themselves in illness, lost a loved one, or suffered from a traumatic event (likely all of us) knows that grief extends well beyond language to include images, fantasies, and dreams—all of which are imbued with emotion. Collectively, these experiences contribute to what has been described as the soul, that intermediary space between what is known through sense perception and the intellect (Romanyshyn, 2007, p. 81). Psychological research needs to reclaim the soul not to replace empiricism but to widen its view, witnessing both what empiricism erases and highlights.

Doing research with soul in mind is what psychologist Robert Romanyshyn described as the goal of alchemical hermeneutics and the wounded researcher. He stated, "Research with soul in mind is re-search, a searching again for something that has already made its claim upon us, something we have already known, however dimly, but have forgotten" (2007, p. 4). The researcher with soul in mind looks for evidence of mourning un-metabolized in her own fantasies and imagery. Emotions then become as significant as thought, since it is through what is felt—and perhaps, more often, what cannot be felt—that the need to mourn is witnessed. As Romanyshyn pointed out, "Re-search that keeps soul in mind must attend to the feeling of mourning for what is left behind in our saying and knowing. Whatever is said must not lose touch with this feeling quality in our knowing" (p. 11). Such an approach, rather than undermining thought, enriches it. To quote Romanyshyn again: "It deepens research and makes it richer by attending to the images in the ideas, the fantasies in the facts, the dreams in reasons, the myths in the meanings" (p. 12).

This monograph follows Romanyshyn's guidelines for alchemical hermeneutics as a research methodology. Hermeneutics is the practice of interpretation as a search for meaning. Typically, hermeneutics relies on rational argumentation and analytical thinking to discover the meaning of texts and events. With alchemical hermeneutics, the soul takes its rightful place as a vital aspect of human interpretation. Rational interpretations of events, texts, and other contexts are joined with the researcher's imagery, dreams, revelations, and complexes in hopes of moving beyond ego intentions to include the soul as a motivating force guiding the research effort. Alchemical hermeneutics is particularly apt for the project of witnessing how dissociation contributes to "forgetting" the human need for emotional connection and soul. As Romanyshyn remarked, "This imaginal approach to research is about the re-collection of what has been forgotten, left behind, neglected, marginalized, and unfinished, and for this reason, it has a place in the city of soul" (2007, p. 87).

A Depth Psychotherapist's Rationale

Jung wrote about the importance of recognizing the psychological impact of societal problems:

> A collective problem, if not recognized as such, always appears as a personal problem, and in individual cases may give the impression that something is out of order in the realm of the personal psyche. The personal sphere is indeed disturbed, but such disturbances need not be primary; they may well be secondary, the consequence of an unsupportable change in the social atmosphere. The cause of disturbance is, therefore, not be sought in the personal surroundings, but rather in the collective situation. Psychotherapy has hitherto taken this matter far too little into account. (as cited in Romanyshyn, 1983, pp. 233–234)

By increasing awareness of how dissociation is both a psychological defense and a response to social conditions, I hope to articulate one of the collective problems that result from living in an emotionally overwhelming society. I also hope to demonstrate how the societal problem of dissociation often ails people who seek psychotherapy, sometimes as much as the personal conditions of their lives. In part, this connection between societal and individual problems is because of soul. As discussed, the soul is collective rather than unitary. When we speak of soul, we refer to an indivisible connection between all human beings. Hence, disturbances in the social realm inevitably impact individual psyches.

A central role of depth psychotherapists is tender of soul. For this relationship, as Hillman remarked, "The I-Thou is a necessity, a given a priori with the gift of soul" (1972, p. 27). The goal of treatment is integration of mind, body, and soul within the context of shared humanity. In contrast, the medical model emphasizes objectivity and a certain emotional reserve that supports analyzing and eradicating pathology. Successful treatment is associated with producing behaviors perceived as "normal" in relation to predominant social norms. However, in a world that increasingly denigrates the basic human need for connection and requires dissociative defenses for emotional survival, returning people to a "normal" state can be a betrayal of soul and a lost opportunity for fostering deep social-emotional bonds.

Tending soul necessitates "I-Thou" connections that validate the whole person without distinctions between the normal and the pathological. Nevertheless, there is attention to the individual's connection with the wider world and its needs. Soul is a phenomena we create and imbibe together, like Indra's net, a thousand points of light connected as one. Opposing the individual to the collective, or denying their mutual influence, ignores the indivisibility of soul. When we attend to soul in one person, we may ignite soul in others as well, and begin to alter the web of humanity. With soul the focus of psychotherapy, more than the individual becomes open to growth and change.

2

EXCAVATING THE SOUL'S ERASURE

Indeed, the primitive world regarded the preservation of first spirit as the greatest, most urgent of all its tasks. It designed elaborate ritual, ceaselessly fashioned myths, legends, stories, and music, to contain the meaning and feed the fire of the creative soul.
— Laurens van der Post, *The Heart of the Hunter*

Stepping outside any dominant perspective can be a challenging, even taxing, process. This is particularly true of the search for the connection between human emotions, the soul, and dissociative defenses in late modern American society. Whereas emotions may be measured and classified, the soul is not amenable to scientific observation and prevailing Western beliefs—one reason it was exiled by the Enlightenment worldview. Similarly, the relationship between emotions and soul defies rationalistic ways of knowing that are honored by science and the medical model.

I imagine the modern relationship with soulful connection is like shifting beliefs about the Pleiades star cluster, those

Seven Sisters of Greek mythology whom Zeus turned into stars to comfort their father, Atlas. I wonder who think of the sisters' fates when they look to the cluster. For some, a connection might be more quickly made to Subaru automobiles. (*Subaru* is the Japanese translation of *Pleiades*.) Like the Pleiades, the original meaning of soul is pushed underground, lost to the present drive for commodification and individualistic needs and desires.

There is another way the soul is like the Pleiades, one that has to do with *perceiving* the star cluster. If you want to see most constellations clearly, you look directly at the stars. For example, if you want to find Orion in the night sky, you scan the horizon for the stars that make up his body, belt, and sword. But if you want to see the Pleiades, you turn your head away, spotting the stars with your peripheral vision. From the corner of your eye, you get the clearest view of the Seven Sisters.

The same is true of soul. If I try to look for soul straight on, through the late modern worldview framing what I can and cannot see, I get a blurry image. The soul is morphed by my well-honed ego, my training as a scientist, my successful survival as an individualist, and my dependency on the separation of the private and public spheres of life for protection of my individual rights. To find the basic human need for soulful connections, I must dig deep into the past to a time when the power of human emotional connection was undeniable. Nevertheless, I begin my search in my own not-too-distant past.

The dissertation I wrote over two decades ago (2000) was an investigation into how a person's sense of personhood changes when psychic suffering is translated through scientific discourse into a mood disorder. I used Foucault's (1984/1990) matrix of experience to describe how deeply personal experiences of distress and alienation can be understood as mood disorders and a generalized form of human suffering. In that project, I witnessed how the soul could be written out of human experience, although I did not identify what was occurring *as* loss of soul. However, I now believe that it was.

In this chapter, I again look to Foucault's matrix of experience. This time, though, my efforts are directed towards reclaiming emotions and the soul. As mentioned in Chapter One, Foucault originally created the matrix of experience to identify the factors contributing to *thought*—the supposed *sine qua non* of the Western experience of selfhood. In contrast, I use the matrix to identify what was written out of human experience by the Enlightenment worldview: the significance of social-emotions bonds that for millions of years were the basis for emerging with community, a sense of self, and soul. I also use the matrix to identify how dissociation has become a common way of relating to self and the world in late modern American society.

Foucault's matrix of experience arose from his archaeology of thought in which one of the goals was to identify the discontinuities between different epochs according to how the experience of being human was objectified through dominant discourses (Foucault, 1971/1972). With a few changes, I believe I can adapt Foucault's project, creating an archaeology for exploring how emotions are configured, manipulated, and expressed—or not expressed—in different epochs. As mentioned, the focus of this monograph is late modern America and how dissociation from emotions and human connection has become a dominant way of surviving a traumatizing world—an emotional strategy that currently threatens the ability to construct social-emotional bonds and emerge with soul. Thus, rather than looking for the construction of self through thought, as Foucault did, I am looking for the erasure of soul, which I believe is witnessed most directly through the erasure of social-emotional bonds.

Like an archaeologist using remote sensing and painstakingly laying a grid before excavating, I use Foucault's matrix of experience to create order in a seemingly incomprehensible scene. Just as the archaeologist imagines past worlds from pottery shards and bits of bone, I, too, try to imagine what has been lost. No doubt, what I yearn to see says as much about my own sense of alienation and limited human connections in my late modern life. Like the archaeologist, I am tempted to project my dreams on a past that cannot speak for itself. There is always the risk of getting caught in Utopian fantasies, hence the power of topologies and grid lines to keep projections in check.

As discussed in Chapter One, according to Foucault's matrix of experience, the three most significant contributors to the complex experience of becoming a "self" in modern Western societies are a *field of knowledge, methods for self-relation,* and a *collection of rules.* I reproduce Foucault's matrix of experience as follows. First, in this chapter, for the field of knowledge, I share research that supports the emerging view that the evolution of human emotions was central to our species' survival. Collectively, this research creates a very different image of what it means to be human than the view of human nature passed down from the Enlightenment.

For a dominant method of self-relation, I share research on dissociation that attests to its role as a defense against emotionally threatening relationships and a sign to others of the need for supportive social-emotional bonds, and possibly, social change.

Then, in Chapter Three, I suggest dissociation has become a common psychological mechanism for enduring emotionally annihilating conditions prevalent in late modern America. Due to a collection of rules that maintain rigid distinctions between public and private spheres of life, late modern America lacks opportunities for dissociation to lead to social transformation, which research suggests it does in societal structures that were more common prior to civilization. This archaeology of emotions aims to reveal how our inner experience of emotions and soul are impacted by the societies and cultures in which we live.

A Field of Knowledge: The Significance of Emotions

The night before I started writing this section, I had the following dream:

> *I am in a job interview at the Jung Institute, sitting before a panel of analysts. I am telling the panel that the brain is inherently symbolic, an outcome of how it has evolved over time. Using the Triune model of the brain, I describe the brain as having three sections: the brain stem, the limbic system, and the cortex. I say that although the three sections are connected, their tendency is to function as separate systems. Each system knows of the others' needs and desires through the human organism's response to symbolic material, which is the epiphenomena we experience through our imaginal world of fantasies and dreams. I stress to the panel that this is proof that at our core, we humans are deeply relational beings—even our brains work relationally. To be in harmony in our inner life, we must be deeply relational in our outer world as well.* (author's dream journal, March 4, 2010)

I believe this was a confessional dream. As a student at Pacifica Graduate Institute, I learned to look for how theorists' personal histories and values informed how they perceived the world and what they chose to study. It is no different with me. I see a lack of social-emotional bonds in late modern America, just as I often experienced weak attachments and a lack of loving kindness in my family of origin. My healing journey has been centered on finding and creating social-emotional bonds based on the inherent worth of all life. Not surprisingly, what I find most painful about late modern America is lack of social-emotional bonds, and the solution I see for our collective problems is better relationships and more community. I look deep into the past to find evidence for what I hold in my heart to be an undeniable truth.

∼

An Archaeological Survey

Although humans are indisputably the dominant predator around the world, understanding how we came to wield so much power involves peering behind the façade of our species' superiority to a time when our ancestors were prey as often as they were predator. Indeed, it is our ancestors' much longer history as prey and ecological misfits that enlightens us about the nature of the human species today.

For perhaps millions of years, humans lived in small clans of no more than 150 people (Clippinger, 2007). These hunter-gatherers lived before agriculture held humans in place, before the Axial Age, when pagan gods gave way to one God, and even before writing was invented in Mesopotamia for the purpose of recording taxes, thereby laying the ground for distinguishing rich from poor (Armstrong, 2001; Radin, 1972). They had little or no possessions and were dependent on one another for survival. Together they roamed to quell their hunger pains. Once they were full and shelter was secured, there was time left to do nothing. They worked only 14 to 16 hours a week (Glendinning, 1994). The rest of their time was likely spent just being together, singing, dancing, telling stories, and making stone tools. Unlike today, there would have been a lot of what is now referred to as "face time"—a distinction that widens the divide between our ancestors' world and ours.

To be human in their universe was not to dominate nature but revere her while being embedded within her. In a world of so few people and so much wilderness, to know oneself was to know another; the two probably often felt indistinguishable. Environmentalist Paul Shepard described these people as:

> That peculiar blend of loyalty and tolerance spanning the gap between separateness and belonging, forming a tapestry of ideas, feelings, speculation, experiences, and body that is ME, related to the multitude out there, from human brothers to the distant stars, that are the Other. (1982, p. 13)

Such an embodied sense of others and self likely affected all aspects of our ancestors' sense of the world. Thoughts, perceptions, feelings, the quality of attention, relationships with others and with deities—even the notion of what could be possessed—were affected by their embedded sense of being in the world.

Their sense of time was different as well. Unlike modern Westerners, the future was not primarily a space to predict or control but the next opportunity in an ever-changing landscape of possibilities in which humans were actors but also equally acted upon. Communities existed within the flux of life, not outside or above it. Like the immature sapling struggling to take hold, our ancestors adapted to changing seasons and conditions to survive.

How can I understand the hunter-gatherer way of life, given my late modern Western lifestyle, which, according to Albert Borgmann, "is not simply the advancement of an age-old human striving for more comfort and security but the mobilization of a peculiar massive aggressiveness that breaks through ancient restraints and reserves" (1992, p. 51)? Does my modern relationship with the natural world blind me to the hunter-gatherer way of life?

I am jotting down my visions of the past on a small table in a Barnes & Noble café in San Jose, California. I have been here before and thus drove here today with a profound sense of certainty that not only would the café be almost identical to when I was here last but that my car would be parked where I had left it the evening before. The road I would take to get here would also still be there, and I could assume the majority of drivers shared the same rules for driving so I would arrive here unscathed. The bookstore would be open at the posted time, with the lights on and the temperature controlled. The latte machine would be working. There would be caramel syrup to add to my coffee, and the encounter with the barista would be pleasant, although contrived. The weather conditions would not be a deterrent to getting to the café. It could be any season, and the bookstore would likely still be standing. The only uncertainty I anticipated was where I might sit, but my favorite table was empty once again.

As I sit here in the café at *my* table, I witness at the next table—a psyche's world away—a woman hugging her giggling child with one hand as her other hand pecks at a computer. Diagonal to me, a man hunches over yet another computer, his ears encased in headphones, his mind, I imagine, encased in email. He is wearing a t-shirt that says, "If I agreed with you, we'd both be wrong!" This is the closest I am getting to social connection this morning.

～

Humans were originally a prey species. As science writer Sharon Begley pointed out, "Being hunted brought evolutionary pressure on our ancestors to cooperate and live in cohesive groups. That, more than aggression and warfare, is our evolutionary legacy" (2007, p. 56). Long before our ancestors became hunter-gatherers, they were solitary primates living in the jungle canopies. It was their failure to compete that led to our species' emergence.

Trouble in paradise bedeviled our earliest ancestors over

five million years ago during a period of global warming not unlike the one we are experiencing today (Turner, 2000). Woodlands and vast grasslands filled the spaces left by receding rainforests. Only the most tenacious species retained a foothold in the few lush jungles that remained. Our primate ancestors were not among them. Instead, they were a scrappy lot and not too keen on each other's company. They spent their days scurrying on all fours along the branches of the forest canopy, leaping from tree to tree in search of fruit. Together time was mainly a sniff and a hoot made in passing, although dominance displays, sex, and caring for young could extend time together. Mothers likely abandoned their babies once they were mature enough to forage on their own.

Monkeys were our ancestors' greatest competitors. Traveling in packs, swiftly brachiating with their long arms from tree limb to tree limb, their approach must have made a formidable sight to the lone ape. Noisily and effortlessly they would swarm a fruit tree and defend it from an isolated primate unskilled in social warfare. Like our ape ancestors, the monkeys' forerunners could use their visual acuity and increased mammalian cortex to identify and distinguish a vast array of fruit and recall the exact time of year each kind would ripen (Turner, 2000).

Monkeys' adaptations to the receding jungles likely accelerated our primate ancestors' exodus to the open savannas. Monkeys developed the ability to digest unripened fruit and grew pouches in their cheeks to hold the food their stomachs were too full to digest (Andrews, 1996; Carroll, 2006). As a group, they could eat a tree bare well before primates arrived at the anticipated time of harvest.

What a dejected bunch our early ancestors must have been, near starvation, with no choice but to leave the treetops and eventually venture beyond the jungle floor. Few survived, but the ones who did found themselves pushed well beyond their comfort zone. On the open savanna, they became prey for large mammals and birds, but perhaps even more challenging was their need to learn to live in groups, to trust one another, and eventually to learn to love (Turner, 2000).

According to the sociologist Jonathan Turner (2000), our distant ancestors' greatest obstacle on the African savanna was not the legendary saber-toothed cat but their propensity for weak emotional bonds and preference for autonomy. Turner theorized that the development of a wide and complex emotional repertoire in conjunction with a greater capacity for memory made it possible to manage an increasing number of relationships and complex social dynamics.

Similarly, the evolutionary biologist Robin Dunbar hypothesized that increased brain size, particularly in the neocortex region, had more to do with managing social relations and less to do with making a smarter ape (Dunbar, 1998). An expanded neocortex meant our species could memorize faces and the ways they expressed emotions. It also meant our ancestors (and later us) could remember who had a relationship with whom and manipulate this information to their own ends. A large neocortex ordained the skill of quickly processing emotional information and, if need be, rapidly responding to the expressed needs of others, a necessary skill for creating bonds and solidarity—not to mention staying alive.

According to Turner, becoming more social did not make us less individualistic. Instead, our ancestors' expanding neocortices altered their fundamental need for autonomy, ironically pronouncing and finessing its expression. A strong sense of self was foundational for the development of deep emotional ties to others. The self became an object shared through emotion. Furthermore, with the awareness of the self came a subtle and profound connection: others had minds too. Emotions became the basis for anticipating one's own actions and the actions of others. The past and the future were born, and with them, consciousness.

The evolution of the human brain has been accidental and fortuitous. What came before remained with minimal alterations. The neuroscientist David Linden compared the brain's evolution to the building of an ice cream cone: "As higher functions were added, a new scoop was placed on top, but the lower scoops were left largely unchanged. In this way, our human brainstem, cerebellum and midbrain are not very different in overall plan from that of a frog" (2007, p. 21). On top of the so-called reptilian brain, a scoop of emotional brain was added, the limbic system, and on top of that, the decision-making neocortex, where cognition is believed to dominate.

While old structures were left largely unchanged, the connections made between each scoop made all the difference. With cognition and emotion interconnected and emotions developing beyond the basics of fear, aggression, and maternal love, humans could tag memories of social interactions and use these connections to solidify relationships and together defend against threats to survival. As Turner contended, "Memory and thought cannot take place without the capacity to tag thoughts, experiences, and emotions with affect. And the more the affective variety possible, the more complex and subtle the cognitive capacities" (2000, pp. 60–61).

According to Turner, lurking in human evolutionary development was the retained potential for autonomy and perhaps one day the return of the lone ape. Turner claimed, "My view is that, at our older ape core, we are individualists who chafe against organizational constraint, but we are also an animal that can use a highly attuned emotional system to create social bonds and to sustain tight-knit social structures" (2000, p. xii).

Yet much has occurred in the five million years since the epoch Turner's theory illuminates, and one change is that the lone ape in us now chafes as much against isolation as it does against membership in the group. As Turner contended, our emotions likely developed for the purpose of communication and group survival, but their emergence also created in us a desire to *feel* with another. Eventually, we began to need the company of others not just for our physical survival but our emotional survival as well. What might have been adaptive to our primate ancestor—solitary living in the jungle's treetops—is devastating for *Homo sapiens sapiens*. Hence, banishment from the group has become one of the most heinous forms of punishment. Primatologist Franz de Waal observed, "Next to death, solitary confinement is our most extreme punishment. Our bodies and minds are not designed for lonely lives. We become hopelessly depressed in the absence of human company, and our health deteriorates" (2005, p. 6). De Waal pointed to primate evolution to support the view of humans as a species with a fundamental need for strong social-emotional bonds:

> Origin stories that neglect this deep connection by presenting humans as loners who grudgingly came together are ignorant of primate evolution. We belong to a category of animals known among zoologists as "obligatorily gregarious," meaning that we have no option but to stick together. This is why fear of ostracism lurks in the corners of every human mind: being expelled is the worst thing that can befall us. It was so in biblical times, and it remains so today. Evolution has instilled a need to belong and to feel accepted. We are social to our core. (pp. 219–220).

Similarly, Jung once wrote, "Man is a herd animal and is only healthy when he lives as a social being" (1933, p. 48).

As our emotional repertoire increased, perhaps our sense of aloneness also became more palpable. Emotions can be overwhelming and create feelings of isolation from others when we cannot understand what they mean. By looking into the face of another or witnessing another's body language, and thus seeing our emotions mirrored back at us, we come to understand the nature of what we are feeling while connecting with another. Through others we give meaning to our experiences and stave off the loneliness that threatens an autonomous being that has become conditioned to living in a group.

I believe that over time humans developed soul through a longing to connect with others. Soul thrives through relationships. Indeed, Jung believed human connection was vital for the soul, remarking, "Soul . . . can live only in and from human relationships . . . the conscious achievement of inner unity clings desperately to human relationships as to an indispensable condition" (as cited in Hillman, 1972, p. 25). Soul deepens our experiences through our connections with others.

Similar to Turner and de Waal, other scientists and researchers are highlighting the need for social-emotional bonds as a central aspect of our evolved nature, which, taken together, might suggest the beginning of a change in societal beliefs and practices. This research contributes to a new field of knowledge of what it means to be human, creating what Foucault might have called an emerging *episteme* in the late modern Western epoch (1966/1970).

Foucault described the episteme as the "*positive unconscious* of knowledge: a level that eludes the scientist's consciousness and yet is part of the scientific discourse" (1966/1970, p. xi). The notion of the episteme is used to stress how "conditions of possibilities"—rather than technologies and theories—order scientific practices, determining such things as what is studied, seen as fact, and expressed through the dominant discourses (p. xxii). An episteme differs from a *paradigm*, a concept introduced by Thomas Kuhn to describe a dominant scientific view in a discipline, which is supported by theories, technologies, practices, and political agendas (1996). (The classic example of a paradigm shift is the replacement of Newtonian physics with Einstein's theory of special relativity.) An episteme functions much more broadly than a paradigm, transcending disciplinary boundaries.

I think the "positive unconsciousness" Foucault (1966/1970) associates with the episteme may be analogous to Jung's perception of the psyche's unconscious, which compensates the ego's conscious attitude. Jung wrote:

> A psychological theory, if it is to be more than a technical makeshift, must base itself on the principle of opposition; for without this it could only re-establish a neurotically unbalanced psyche. There is no balance, no system of self-regulation, without opposition. The psyche is just such a self-regulating system. (as cited in Storr, 1983, p. 167).

Perhaps science also can be a self-regulating system like the psyche. If so, the research I discuss in the next section (and the vast amount of work that reaches similar conclusions) may be a collective, unconscious attempt to reorder human experience to include our need for deep emotions and social bonds. I certainly hope this is true.

An Emerging Episteme

The Zulus have a saying: *a person is a person through other persons*. Late modern Western science is starting to catch up with this ancient tribal wisdom in fields such as neuroscience, psychology, anthropology, philosophy, primatology, and even economics. This research points to an understanding of the nature of human beings as fundamentally social and emotional.

For example, research in neuroscience reveals humans are first and foremost hardwired for relationships. Psychologist

Louis Cozolino even called the brain our "social organ," an idea that first emerged in the 1970s when scientists began mapping the neural circuitry associated with social behavior (2006, p. 11). According to Cozolino:

> For human babies survival doesn't depend on how fast they can run, whether they can climb a tree, or if they can tell the difference between edible and poisonous mushrooms. Rather, they survive based on the abilities of their caretakers to detect the needs and intentions of those around them. For humans, other people are our primary environment. (p. 13)

The human propensity and need for relationships are witnessed in the development of the human brain. In the earliest years of life, the development of the brain's right hemisphere dominates, producing much more neuronal growth than the left hemisphere. The right hemisphere has been described by Jungian analyst Margaret Wilkinson (2006) as "fundamentally associative and relational" (p. 21) and "densely interconnected with limbic regions and therefore contains the major circuitry of emotional regulation" (p. 9). Through the relationship with the primary caregiver, the infant's right hemisphere develops, coinciding with the development of attachment bonds that emerge through emotional communication. The relationship also fosters neuronal growth in the right hemisphere, giving rise to empathy, emotional regulation, a sense of humanness, and the ability to engage in inner subjective processes (p. x).

The significance of early attachment for the development of the brain is witnessed in children who through neglect fail to receive the love and attention so vital for human development. One study of Romanian orphans who had minimal human contact and spent most of their days alone in their cots showed virtually no neuronal growth in their right orbital frontal

LAURA K KERR, PHD

cortex, an area responsible for integrating communication
throughout the brain, including the limbic area responsible for
emotional regulation (Wilkinson, 2006, p. 22). Similarly,
Wilkinson shared that dissociation "is best understood . . . in
terms of loss of connectivity within the right hemisphere" (p. 9).
Thus, the brain's development appears to mirror the quality of
the relationships the infant is experiencing. If the infant feels
supported in their development, the brain will also be
supported, developing interconnectedness between its regions,
including the limbic system involved in emotional regulation.
However, without relationships to sustain growth, the brain
will fail to make the associative connections necessary for
emotional well-being.

A very different line of research in neuroscience is also
contributing to an emerging episteme that identifies sociality as
a primary characteristic of the human species. The serendipitous discovery of the mirror-neuron system by neuroscientist
Giacomo Rizzolatti and his colleagues has led to extensive
research of the extent to which humans and other primates
learn by imitating others (Rizzolatti & Craighero, 2004). This
research also points to our innate capacity for empathy. Mirror
neurons, first discovered in the premotor cortex of monkeys,
fire even when the action is performed by another and only
observed. For example, Jack watches Jill lift a cup of coffee to
her mouth and take a drink. In Jack's brain, motor neurons in
his premotor cortex fire as if he had taken the drink himself.
Rizzolatti and colleagues observed, "The pattern of neuron
activity associated with the observed action was a true representation in the brain of the act itself, regardless of who was
performing it" (2006, p. 56).

The mirror-neuron system has also been shown to function in emotional interactions and is potentially the basis of
not only grasping others' feelings and moods but also sharing
them. Research conducted at University College showed this

was true for pain (Nash, 2007). Just thinking that a loved one's hand is being electrically shocked was enough to stimulate brain areas that would have responded if the subject's hand had been shocked. Furthermore, an experiment conducted by Bruno Wicker and colleagues (2003) showed that when study participants inhaled something that smelled obnoxious, causing a response of disgust (in this case, butyric acid, found in rancid butter and vomit), or they watched an actor pretend to smell something disgusting, in each scenario the same aspects of the olfactory area of the brain were activated (the anterior insula). The researchers concluded, "There is a common mechanism for understanding the emotion in others and feeling the same emotions in ourselves" (2003, p. 661).

The idea that mirror neurons are the basis of emotional empathy has widely been accepted within the neuroscience community, and some suggest a deficiency in the mirror-neuron system may be a central aspect of autism, a brain disorder characterized by withdrawal from social interaction. Autism is also associated with a limited ability to be self-reflectively aware of one's own mind or the minds of others. It may well be that the capacity to conceive of mental events in oneself and others makes possible intersubjectivity and meaningful relationships.

According to neuroscientists Vilayanur Ramachandran and Lindsay Oberman, "Mirror neurons may enable humans to see themselves as others see them, which may be an essential ability for self-awareness and introspection" (2006, p. 65). In fact, "People with autism show reduced mirror neuron activity in the inferior frontal gyrus, a part of the brain's premotor cortex, perhaps explaining their inability to assess the intentions of others" (p. 65). Like the initial development of the right hemisphere of the human brain in response to relationships, mirror neurons also seem to facilitate social-emotional bonds.

Without them, humans appear to have limited ability to emotionally connect with others.

Another line of research supporting the emerging episteme emphasizing humans' propensity for creating social-emotional bonds comes from the work of psychologist Paul Eckman (2003). Eckman used ethnographic fieldwork to identify the universal expression of several basic human emotions, including happiness, anger, disgust, and sadness. Eckman studied people from cultures all over the world, including an isolated aboriginal group in New Guinea who, at the time of the study, had no exposure to Western culture. By asking his subjects to make up stories about people in the photographs he shared, Eckman demonstrated that all people, irrespective of their cultural origins, associated the same facial expressions with happiness, anger, disgust, and sadness. Furthermore, research has shown that congenitally blind people spontaneously make the expected facial expressions for these emotions. Eckman remarked:

> If expressions do not need to be learned, then those who are born congenitally blind should manifest similar expression to those of sighted individuals. A number of studies have been done over the past sixty years, and repeatedly that is what has been found, especially for spontaneous facial expression. (p. 14)

Turner (2000) identified one of the most profound consequences of having universal facial expressions: difficulty denying not only others' emotions but also what we are truly feeling. "There are constraints imposed by the neurological and body systems activating different emotions, and while it is possible to be delusional, defensive, and deceitful (to oneself and others), it is difficult to call anger another emotion" (p. 126). While there may be a social structure, or *habitus*, guiding which emotions are appropriate to express (e.g., crying at a funeral is okay in most cultures, while laughing hysterically is not), the activation of basic emotions such as anger, happiness, disgust, and sadness occurs outside our control. This is not surprising, since the need to read facial expressions accurately is supported by what is known about the development of the right hemisphere for attachment and the presence of a mirror neuron system. Through reading and producing facial expressions, the developing child learns how to live within a society according to its prescribed norms for creating social-emotional bonds.

Typically, the family is the first "society" a child encounters, learning from her caregivers' facial expressions what makes them happy, possibly leading to positive interactions, and what makes them angry, potentially leading to punishment. Through facial displays of disgust, children learn what not to eat, and through expressions of sadness they become acquainted with emotional pain. Yet children produce these emotional expressions as well, and their parents' response sets the stage for which emotions a child will learn are validated and supported in her world and which will be disallowed or denied (Linehan, 1993).

Emotional invalidation is often the norm for children who grow up in households where adverse experiences predominate (Linehan, 1993). *Adverse childhood experiences* include recurrent physical abuse; recurrent emotional abuse; sexual abuse; an alcohol and/or drug abuser in the household; an incarcerated household member; living with someone who is chronically depressed, mentally ill, institutionalized, or suicidal; domestic violence; an absence of one or both parents; and emotional and physical neglect (Anda et al., 2004).

Based on self-reports of over 17,000 adults for a study conducted by Southern California Kaiser Permanente and the Center for Disease Control and Prevention, it was learned that more than two-thirds of the participants in the study had at least one adverse childhood experience while growing up; over two-fifths had a history of at least two of these experiences (Anda et al., 2004). Similar results were obtained from a study conducted at the University of Minnesota, Twin Cities. Psychologists Frazier, Gavian, Perera, and Anders (2007) administered the Traumatic Life Events questionnaire to 1,528 college students. From the students' responses, Frazier and colleagues learned that 85% had experienced at least one trauma in their relatively short lives, and on average students reported a history of three traumas. The most common traumatic events included sudden bereavement (47%), life-threatening illness of a family member or friend (30%), witnessing family violence (23%), receiving unwanted sexual attention (21%), and involvement in an accident in which either the student or someone else was hurt (19%). The long-term impact of adverse childhood experiences and early trauma is far reaching, leading to depression, anxiety, and other mental disorders; cancer, obesity, lung disease, and other health problems; and attachment disorders and difficulty trusting love (Chapmana et al., 2004; Felitti et al., 1998; Lyons-Ruth et al., 2006). Thus, if "normal" correlates with the greatest number of people, then coming from a normal household in America means growing up in conditions that lead to poor emotional and physical health in adulthood.

In the presence of adverse childhood experiences, a child may naturally feel angry or sad, yet their feelings may be ignored or denied, or the child may even be told to stop expressing their emotions. *"Don't you cry"* is not an uncommon response when a caregiver is unwilling or unable to validate a child's emotions. In the most emotionally painful circumstances, such as when abuse is present or a child is frightened of the caregiver, children may attempt to express no emotions at all if they believe this will keep them safe. Herman noted that when abused children observe signs of danger, they often tried to become inconspicuous, including keeping their faces expressionless (1997). Not only are their efforts directed towards basic survival, but their sense of survival is also deeply emotional. As Herman contended, "All of the abused child's psychological adaptations serve the fundamental purpose of preserving her primary attachments to her parents in the face of daily evidence of their malice, helplessness, or indifference" (p. 102).

Imagine how different children's experiences are in cultures where adverse childhood experiences are not the norm. Jean Liedloff, a writer who conducted ethnographic work with the Yequana Indians of the Amazon rainforest, witnessed childrearing in this so-called *Stone Age* culture (1985). Liedloff developed the notion of the *continuum concept* to describe what she believed was the natural and adaptive way of raising children that emerged over the millions of years humans lived as hunter-gatherers. According to the continuum concept, human development reflects innate expectations for a particular environment, in particular, the social environment we are adapted to inhabit:

> The expectation of taking part in a culture is a product of our evolution and the mores that are seized upon by that expectation are, when assimilated, as integral a component of our personalities as the inborn ways of other species. (p. 40)

Liedloff identified one aspect of childrearing that seemed invariable among the Yequana but largely absent in the United States: Yequana caregivers constantly held infants until they developed the need to roam freely. Liedloff believed the Yequanas' habit of honoring their children's innate timeline for developing independence contributed to the general sense of wellbeing witnessed not only in the children but also in the adult members of the tribe. Liedloff argued that Western practices for childrearing, which emphasize independence at the earliest possible time, are contrary to humans' innate developmental needs, which over millions of years have centered on developing healthy attachment rather than preternatural independence. Liedloff felt the emphasis on independence in America led to emotional suffering for both mother and infant: "The violent tearing apart of the mother-child continuum, so strongly established during the phases that took place in the womb, may understandably result in depression for the mother, as well as agony for her infant" (1985, p. 36).

If denying the opportunity to be held can have such dire consequences, how impactful could it be to have other emotional needs denied or ignored, or worse, to be frightened of one's caretakers, which characteristically occurs when abuse is present? According to Liedloff, "There are neuroses and insanities to protect the deprived from the brunt of unmeetable reality. There is a numbness that overtakes pain beyond bearing" (1985, p. 48).

In the next section, I will discuss dissociation as one of the ways the mind defends against the failure to have innate needs for protection and connection met. Like Liedloff, I believe much of the "pain beyond bearing" in the United States can be associated with unmet attachment needs and an overemphasis on independence, as well as emotionally traumatizing experiences.

A Method of Self-Relation: Dissociation

Foucault depicted methods of self-relation as those aspects of the matrix of experience that lead to the construction of a sense of self as a subject of particular discourses (1984/1990). Foucault believed discourses and their associated practices model for individuals how they can—or cannot—relate to themselves in order to recognize themselves as members of a society. In many regards, aligning oneself with a society's dominant discourses is a way to avoid alienation while creating solidarity with others who are similarly identified. Foucault claimed that, although all are obliged to interact with their society's dominant discourses in the creation of selfhood, these discourses are not necessarily oppressive. In his later works, he described methods of self-relation as "technologies of the self" through which life can be constructively created:

> Technologies of the self . . . permit individuals to effect by their own means, or with the help of others, a certain number of operations on their own bodies and souls, thoughts, conduct, and way of being, so as to transform themselves in order to attain a certain state of happiness, purity, wisdom, perfection, or immortality. (1988, p. 18)

For Foucault, technologies of the self involve intentional efforts to acquire prescribed skills and attitudes. While this is a reasonable assumption for how selfhood is created when the goal of research is to elaborate an archaeology of thought, an archaeology of emotions needs to pay attention to innate qualities and predispositions, thereby mirroring the nature of emotions. For an archaeology of emotions, searching for technologies of the self and other methods of self-relation is still relevant, but rather than identifying practices of reason or thought, the goal is to look for adaptive, *unintentional* technologies initially outside a person's control. However, the final objective for both archaeologies is the same: to discover how efforts at creating a self occur in response to a particular culture or society.

For an archaeology of thought and an archaeology of emotions, the matrix of experience depicts how a person becomes a self within a society or culture, yet they differ in what they perceive as most relevant to understanding selfhood and the creation of a dominant episteme. For Foucault, who was more interested in selfhood emerging through Enlightenment discourses, an archaeology of thought is an appropriate objective. However, I believe we are entering a new era, which some have called the *postmodern*, others have called *the global age*, and still others *late modernity* (Beck, 1999). Regardless of the era's name, a break with the Enlightenment-inspired ways of becoming a self has emerged. Emotions are once again becoming central to how we understand what it means to be human. Perhaps as a result of a long history of not paying attention to emotions, a "positive unconscious," as Foucault described epistemes, is emerging (Foucault, 1966/1970). Yet recovering emotions is not wholly a transparent process. It also involves identifying how we have acquired "technologies" and other methods of self-relation to overcome emotionally untenable situations and retain hope for the "happiness, purity, wisdom, perfection, or immortality" that Foucault associated with technologies of self (1988, p. 18).

In the next three sections, I discuss dissociation as one of the emotion-driven technologies of the self that keep people emotionally connected with others and their own efforts to become a self when they endure emotionally threatening, and sometimes life-threatening, circumstances or environments. My objective is to review some of the literature that supports an understanding of dissociation as a method of self-relation contributing to our ability to maintain social-emotional bonds.

My past plays a significant role in the literature I have chosen to share. My personal experiences with dissociation arose in response to childhood abuse. I believe my ability to dissociate from traumatic events led to a blunting of emotional experience and expression, but this, I believe, was a relatively small price to pay since it allowed me to stay emotionally connected to my parents. Through dissociation, I remained a member of my tribe, my family. In the rest of this chapter, I share literature that supports my experience of dissociation's function and also points to how my experience is shared by many.

History of the Concept of Dissociation

The word *dissociation* first became a psychiatric concept in the late nineteenth century through the work of the French psychotherapist Pierre Janet (Hacking, 1995). Janet used the term to explain the psychological characteristics of his patients diagnosed with hysteria, or *hysterics,* as they were once called. The diagnosis of hysteria, which no longer exists, was almost singularly given to women—especially single women who were thought to shun men. According to historian Elizabeth Lunbeck, "Hysteria was a malady suffered by undersexed prudes in a sexualized world" (1994, p. 212). Yet for many of these women—the majority of whom had been victims of incest, rape, or other forms of sexualized assault—symptoms of hysteria "represented a dramatic protest against the general cultural precept that the woman's body was fair game" (p. 212). Janet was the first to observe that the primary pathologies hysterics suffered were the aftereffects of a traumatic event that had occurred in their pasts. Janet introduced the term *dissociation* to identify the pathological state of being unable to integrate memories of emotionally overwhelming events (Herman, 1997).

When Janet wrote about dissociation in the late nineteenth century, self-awareness was considered a fundamental characteristic of mental health (van der Kolk et al., 1996). Having memories of past events would be significant for self-awareness. According to Janet, hysterics suffered because of the nature of traumatic memories, which kept them from becoming self-aware. Janet identified two types of memory, *traumatic memory* and *narrative memory*. Janet depicted narrative memory as our commonsense form of memory—that straightforward capacity to narrate past events—whereas traumatic memory was defined as the unconscious repetition of lasting physiological changes that result from trauma, including "intense emotions but without clear memory of the event" (Herman, 1997, p. 34). The term *dissociation* was thus used to describe memories split from consciousness, appearing to be forgotten yet remembered unconsciously through the body and emotions. The result, according to Janet, was that hysterics had "an illness of the personal synthesis" that kept them from forming an integrated sense of self (as cited in Dorahy & van der Hart, 2007).

Philosopher and historian Ian Hacking described the nineteenth century as a time when "memory became a surrogate for spiritual understanding of the soul" (1995, p. 197). Terms like *trauma* and *dissociation* were a central aspect of the shift from a spiritual understanding of suffering to a science of memory. Through a science of memory, sinful behavior became the product of events rather than the result of poor character:

> The psychologicalization of trauma is an essential part of that structure, because the spiritual travail of the soul, which so long served as a previous ontology, could now become hidden psychological pain, not the result of sin that seduces us within, but caused by the sinner outside who seduces us. Trauma was a pivot upon which this revolution turned. (p. 197).

Around the same time, William James defined trauma as "thorns in the spirit." James was also responsible for introducing the term *dissociation* into the American vernacular (Hacking, 1995).

The idea of dissociation and traumatic memories was used to formulate the diagnosis of multiple personality disorder, when entire personalities split off from memory (Hacking, 1995). Dissociation also became associated with the psychological aftereffects of combat (van der Kolk et al., 1996). However, as has been the case with much research on trauma during the past century, Janet's work was virtually forgotten at times, along with the idea of psychological trauma being the origin of mental disturbances.

Jung was one psychiatrist who elaborated on the work of Janet during the early twentieth century. Jung wrote his dissertation on the psychogenesis of spiritual phenomena, which he described as "psychic dissociation" (1961/1989, p. 322). Jung became interested in dissociation as a psychological phenomenon while attending séances orchestrated by his cousin Helene Preiswork, who was the medium for these events (Jung, 2009). During the séances, Preiswork would appear possessed and become different personalities. Jung was fascinated by these shifts in personalities and other hitherto unexplainable phenomena, such as automatic writing. Jung's understanding of dissociation was formulated in response to these paranormal events, and he brought a psychological lens to the subject. According to Jung, the nature of psychic dissociation can be understood as follows: "In most cases where a split-off complex manifests itself it does so in the form of a personality, as if the complex had a consciousness of itself. Thus, the voices heard by the insane are personified" (1961/1989, p. 322). Jung also witnessed the connection between trauma and dissociation:

> As a result of some psychic upheaval whole tracts of our being can plunge back into the unconscious and vanish from the surface for years and decades . . . disturbances caused by affects are known technically as phenomena of dissociation, and are indicative of a psychic split. (as cited in Wilkinson, 2006, p. xi).

Interest in dissociation, along with multiple personalities, waned during the twentieth century. It resurfaced during the World Wars but did not become steady until the 1970s. With the political mobilization of Vietnam veterans and the origination of the feminist movement, dissociation and Janet's work regained relevance and played a central role in understanding the psychological suffering of combat survivors, victims of sexual assault and domestic violence, and children who had endured abuse and neglect (Herman, 1997). Eventually, post-traumatic stress disorder (PTSD) and a spectrum of dissociative disorders received recognition in the *Diagnostic and Statistical Manual of Mental Disorders (DSM)* as bona fide mental disorders (van der Kolk et al., 1996). The *DSM-IV-TR* defined dissociative disorders as involving "a disruption in the usually integrated functions of consciousness, memory, identity, or perception" (American Psychiatric Association, 2008, p. 519). This classification includes dissociative identity disorder, distinguished by two or more distinct personalities, a designation that replaced the diagnosis of multiple personality disorder.

Today, dissociation has reclaimed scientific prominence. It is the subject of journals (*Dissociation* and *Journal of Trauma and Dissociation*) and a professional society (*International Society for the Study of Trauma and Dissociation*). Research on dissociation tends to fall into four categories: 1) dissociation's occurrence with exposure to traumatic stress, 2) dissociation's association with changes in the personality structure, 3) dissociative phenomena, and 4) the nature of dissociation (Dorahy & van der Hart, 2007). Dissociation is also understood as a common response to stress, which may or may not lead to a full-blown dissociative disorder or PTSD. It has been defined as existing on a continuum and is sometimes depicted as a normal part of everyday existence (Steinberg & Schnall, 2000).

Studies conducted by psychiatrist Marlene Steinberg suggest that "dissociative episodes are very common among normal people even when they're not in any danger" and are typically reactions to overwhelming feelings of stress (Steinberg & Schnall, 2000, p. 12). When generally defined, dissociation may be thought of as the escape when there is no escape. Steinberg observed the following in her "normal" study participants:

> They felt as if they had to escape, and they did it by detaching themselves from their body or the world around them in much the same way that a person in an auto accident or some other cataclysmic situation goes out-of-body or sees the environment as unreal [two experiences commonly identified as dissociative]. (p. 12)

Similarly, psychologist Peter Levine, who studied the somatic aspects of dissociation, asserted that even denial might be "a lower-level energy form of dissociation" (1997, p. 141). Through denial, Levine believed we avoid distressing feelings such as fear, shame, anger, and sorrow, compartmentalizing experiences and the associated emotions that seem too painful to deal with in the moment. This idea suggests that there are adaptive aspects of dissociating during periods of overwhelming stress. In the next section, I share literature that addresses the evolution of dissociation's adaptive traits.

The Evolution of Dissociation

Many natural science museums in the United States have used dioramas to portray assumedly common scenes in the lives of our distant ancestors. Depending on the era depicted, replicas of our ancestors are either covered with thick hair or wearing animal skins. A group of them are usually shown traversing the savanna, huddling around a fire, or perhaps resting by the mouth of a faux cave. Replicas of the more recent past usually show our ancestors carrying stone tools and other implements, suggesting fledgling cognitive capacities and more human-like traits. Saber-tooth cats or woolly mammoths are sometimes painted on the diorama walls, a chilling reminder of the necessity of a cunning mind for surviving a world filled with life-threatening danger.

Despite their generally kitschy feel, these models of our ancestral past capture present sentiments about human evolution and how we make sense of our present behaviors. For example, Peter Levine's somatic understanding of the human response to traumatic events is derived from an understanding of the mammalian reaction to being pursued and attacked by a predator. In such instances, having the capacity to "freeze" (dissociation) not only anesthetizes the animal from the pain of being eaten alive but also allows for the possibility of escape if the predator, resting before eating its kill, thinks the prey is actually dead—thus creating the perfect second chance for escape and survival (1997). Our hominid ancestors would have needed this innate capacity as prey of the saber-tooth cat.

Psychologist Richard McNally seems to pull directly from the natural museum diorama in his arguments against the possibility of forgetting traumatic events such as childhood sexual abuse (2003). McNally can identify no evolutionary value to forgetting trauma. On the contrary, he argues that natural selection favors remembering trauma, since this would have enabled our ancestors to anticipate potentially life-threatening circumstances before they occurred. According to McNally:

> One can easily imagine that natural selection would have favored a capacity to remember trauma. Our ancestors who remembered life-threatening situations they had survived would have been more likely to avoid similar dangers in the future than those who failed to remember them. Indeed,

what is difficult to imagine is how something as maladaptive as a mechanism for repressing, dissociating, or otherwise forgetting trauma could possibly have evolved throughout the course of natural history. (p. 62)

McNally's assumptions make perfect sense if one ascribes to the view of human evolution as driven primarily by increased cognitive abilities and self-preserving behaviors such as fight-or-flight responses. However, when our projections on the past shift to include research that identifies emotional intersubjectivity as a central aspect of human experience and our survival as a species, dissociation and forgetting trauma not only make sense but also may have been necessary for the evolution of culture.

McNally (2003) and Levine (1997) correctly pointed to the role of a hostile environment driving natural selection. However, with regard to dissociation, social hostilities also likely played a significant role in the need to forget trauma. Although it is tempting for me to imagine that our hunter-gatherer ancestors inhabited idyllically peaceful social worlds supporting harmonious relationships, research in anthropology and primatology suggests this was not the case (de Waal, 2005). In all societies, power and social dominance are present and managed through rituals, laws, or institutions. Besides being innately adaptive for empathy, humans are also hardwired for another undeniable aspect of our universal character: the quest for power and status. According to de Waal, "We are born to strive for status" (p. 79). Although our hunter-gatherer ancestors likely experienced a lot less violence than we do today, they also had much less to compete for and fight over.

The pursuit of power and status is as fundamental to human nature as bipedalism and is present in all forms of society, including such groups as the Intuit, Navajo Indians, and

LAURA K KERR, PHD

!Kung San—all noted for their egalitarian social structures (De Waal, 2005). In smaller, egalitarian societies, the quest for status and power is systematically undermined, reducing the formation of steep social hierarchies. De Waal shared the following example of how attempts at domination are dealt with in egalitarian societies:

> Men trying to dominate others are systematically undermined, and male pride is frowned upon. The proverbial fish tale is considered improper. Upon returning to his village, the successful hunter simply sits down in front of his hut without a word. He lets the blood on the shaft speak for itself. Any hint of boasting will be punished with jokes and insults about his miserable catch. (pp. 74–75)

The quest for status and power can be dangerous. Not only is death a possibility, but overwhelming stress is also a common outcome. For our survival, we have become sensitive to the emotions and body language associated with power dynamics and hierarchical differences in power. De Waal claimed our concerns for power are even hardwired into our facial expressions, noting, "The human smile derives from an appeasement signal, which is why women generally smile more than men. In myriad ways, our behavior, even at its friendliest, hints at the possibility of aggression" (2005, p. 82).

De Waal believed sensitivity to power is essential for living in all societies, since social stability requires a clear sense of social order:

> Not only are we sensitive to hierarchies and the body language associated with them, we simply could not live without them. Some people may wish them away, but harmony requires stability, and stability depends ultimately on a well-acknowledged social order. (2005, p. 59)

The question, then, is not whether power and hierarchies are present but how power and status are distributed and dealt with in a society. Preferably, intense struggles are minimized along with extreme differences in power through rituals, such as derisive remarks to boastful hunters, or through judicious rules, which, ideally, is the advantage of democratic societies.

Psychological mechanisms also contribute to managing the overwhelming stress associated with the quest for status and power. The evolution of dissociation in the human species may have included adaptation to power struggles—and perhaps, more often, the experience of defeat. Psychiatrist Horacio Fabrega identified social and environmental pressures enforcing dissociation as an adaptive response to overwhelmingly stressful events (2002). Like Levine (1997), Fabrega thought dissociation emerged as a defense reaction to being prey and included such behaviors as freezing and tonic immobility, which he described as the "phylogenetic precursors to dissociation as a human mental capacity" (p. 296). Thus, the innate, physiological response to being hunted and eaten later changed to assist humans whose emotional survival felt as precarious as the experience of being hunted.

Fabrega associated our modern, Western conception of dissociation with notions of *trance* and *possession* that have been prevalent throughout human history and continue to play a role in non-Western societies. According to Fabrega, trance and possession are ritualized forms of dissociation that *communicate* a person's social-related distress (2002). Fabrega's hypothesis suggests dissociation is more than just a defense against trauma and overwhelming stress; it is also a way for members of a social group to identify when a person has become too overwhelmed by stress, including the threat of social alienation that can arise from the quest for status and power. Fabrega wrote:

> States of dissociation provided inner spaces or psychological arenas in which those stresses tied to psychopathology could be worked out by channeling psychological experience in a positive, conflict-alleviating direction and by producing scenarios of behavior that communicated the distress and played out ways that were safe and culturally understandable, and capable of eliciting sympathy and support. (2002, p. 311)

Supporting Fabrega's ideas, Levine stated that shamans, who often treat trance and possession, recognize the very social nature of these dissociative responses: "Shamanistic cultures view illness and trauma as a problem for the entire community" (1997, p. 57). Levine also identified "rape of the soul" as the most common illness treated by shamanic healers, an illness resulting from overwhelming stress that literally causes the soul to leave the body. Rape of the soul is more likely to be associated with trance states, which, Fabrega claimed, "arise in situations of psychological distress, social conflict, and social marginality" (2002, p. 307). Thus, shamanic treatment is a vital method for reuniting members of the group when social conflicts threaten social cohesiveness.

Possession, however, seems to work differently, and like dissociative identity disorder, it may be a way to communicate the victimhood engendered by social inequalities that have become ingrained aspects of society, such as gender oppression. Spirit possession may be a way for the subjugated and oppressed to voice their realities without fear of retribution, particularly when possession is aligned with religious or spiritual practices. Anthropologist Sherrill Mulhern observed possession functioning as "a theater for voicing frustrations and grievances in male-dominated societies, or as a coercive tool used by women to secure retribution and revenge" (1991, p. 777).

In the United States, possession seems very similar to dissociative identity disorder, especially considering the diagnosis is overwhelmingly given to women (nine out of 10 diagnoses) and, as some argue, is the outcome of a patriarchal society that has historically given men control over the members of a dependent, and potentially isolated, family (Butler, 1996; Chesler, 1989). Rather than religious institutions, those diagnosed with dissociative identity disorders, like hysterics before them, retreat to the mental health system to speak of experiences of hurt and humiliation.

Fabrega witnessed how trance and possession became aligned with different social institutions. He observed:

> Ritualized forms of dissociation like trance and possession are found in association with religious and medical practices across the world and are thus institutionalized in the society. Indeed, one can classify societies in terms of whether institutionalized forms of dissociation are predominantly trance, possession, or a combination of the two. (2002, p. 298)

Interestingly, in the United States we appear to associate these two distinct ways of dealing with overwhelming social distress with one institution: the modern mental health system. Nevertheless, the mental health system continues to uphold two conceptions of extreme traumatic responses—PTSD and dissociative identity disorder—which may retain the distinction between trance and possession, albeit without the corrective community support needed to actually alleviate social-bound distress and conflict.

I hypothesize that when dissociative responses are not relieved through sanctioned social channels, or at least witnessed within a communal context, the otherwise normal response to social distress risks becoming an exaggerated part of the individual's sense of identity or a predominant coping mechanism that indiscriminately gets applied to all experiences of stress. At such times, and in societies that lack opportunities to overcome dissociative defenses, dissociation becomes pathological. Indeed, Fabrega identified dissociation as a precursor to all mental pathology.

The predominance of unresolved dissociative defenses may indicate the level of fragmentation and alienation occurring within a social group. The need for continual reliance on dissociative defenses for emotional survival also likely contributes to a lack of solidarity and social cohesion. The impact of unresolved dissociative defenses may also extend to the next generation, particularly when the parents of developing infants are dissociative (and shut down) or abuse their infants, who, like their parents in late modern America, have no social resources to help them return their souls to their bodies. In the next section, I share research that shows dissociation becomes a normative way of dealing with traumatic stress when the maternal caretaker was emotionally overwhelmed.

Dissociation and Human Development

Not all people with trauma in their pasts dissociate. Furthermore, some individuals without known histories of trauma can sometimes dissociate (Putnam, 1997). To explain this discrepancy, researchers have looked to the first years of life, when infants are initially forming attachments with their caregivers. Evidence suggests that the capacity to dissociate likely arises in conditions of extreme detachment, such as the death of the primary caretaker, or when infants experience their caregivers as emotionally unresponsive to their needs (Lyons-Ruth et al., 2006). Several conditions have been identified as experienced by infants as emotionally unresponsive, including having a frightened caregiver (signaling a dangerous environment), having a frightening (and potentially abusive) caregiver, having a depressed mother, and having a mother with a history of trauma (Lyons-Ruth et al., 2006). These conditions lead to what has been referred to as a disorganized pattern of infant attachment (Bowlby, 1973). According to Lyons-Ruth and colleagues, "Disorganized attachment patterns constitute an initial step in the developmental trajectories that leave an individual vulnerable to developing dissociation in response to later experiences of trauma" (2006, p. 64).

Using a longitudinal study of 126 children from birth to age 19, Lyons-Ruth and colleagues found a connection between disorganized attachment and later development of dissociation (2006). Their study showed that the highest correlation existed between disorganized attachment and later dissociation—even greater than the relationship between dissociation and traumatic events. When mothers were psychologically unavailable, frightening, or frightened during the first 24 months of an infant's life, the likelihood of later dissociation was the greatest. Lyons-Ruth and colleagues concluded, "Disorganization of attachment may be more central to the development of dissociation than the trauma itself" (2006, p. 66).

Another study, conducted by Ogawa, Sroufe, Weinfield, Carlson, and Egeland (1997), showed that the mother's psychological state—rather than the infant's disorganized attachment pattern—determined the likelihood of later dissociation. Lyons-Ruth and colleagues compared the results of their study to the work of Ogawa and colleagues and concluded, "The pathways toward adult dissociative symptoms seem more heavily influenced by the potentially enduring context of disrupted forms of parent-child communication than by the early vulnerability to mental segregation indexed by the infant's disorganized attachment behaviors" (2006, p. 67). Thus, the greatest indicator of later dissociation is a lack of affective communication. This conclusion is supported by research shared earlier in this chapter that emphasized how the evolution and survival of the human species depended on our capacity to form social-emotional bonds.

Summary

This chapter initiated an archaeology of emotions to explore how dissociation has become a common response to overwhelming stress, trauma, and social strain in late modern American society. With Foucault's matrix of experience organizing the excavation, a newly emerging *field of knowledge* and episteme were identified. This episteme portrays the human need for social-emotional bonds as the defining trait of the human species, rather than our rational, cognitive capacities, as the Enlightenment worldview once claimed. This chapter also identified research on dissociation that showed this psychological defense mechanism is foremost a response to failures to establish or maintain social-emotional bonds. Dissociation was described as a *method of self-relation*, which Foucault defined as the ways we relate to ourselves as both individuals and members of a group.

In the next chapter, I look at the third and final aspect of Foucault's matrix of experience contributing to the experience of selfhood, the *collection of rules* governing possibilities. There I will make the argument that dissociation has become a predominant mode of self-relation as a result of the avoidance of social-emotional bonds and the failure to utilize dissociation as a potentially transformative mechanism for social change. In late modern America, the dominant collection of rules governing selfhood contributes to a sharp distinction between the private and public spheres of life, challenging the basic human need for social-emotional bonds. America's Enlightenment-inspired democracy has led to an experience of selfhood in which dissociation has become an unintended defense against soul.

3

DISSOCIATION AS DEFENSE AGAINST SOUL

The primitive spirit stands in rags and tatters, rejected by the contemporary mind, offering us such warnings. Laughing, unaware of peril, we lift the lids of our own particular baskets and, blindly declaring them to be empty, we lose our soul.

— Laurens van der Post, *The Heart of the Hunter*

I have been using Foucault's matrix of experience to create an archaeology of human emotions. The purpose of my excavation has been to explore the psychological conditions of late modern America from the perspective of millions of years of human evolution. As stated, I believe America's inheritance of Enlightenment values, particularly the exaltation of reason and the denigration of emotions, has had a corrosive effect on our psyches, relationships, families, and communities. The basic need for social-emotional bonds was ignored in the creation of American democracy, resulting in social environments characterized by overwhelming stress and social strain—just the conditions in which dissociative defenses are activated and flourish.

In this chapter, I examine the third aspect of Foucault's matrix of experience, the *collection of rules* that contribute to selfhood. With this third facet of Foucault's analysis, my archaeology of emotions intersects with his archaeology of thought. The archaeologies meet where civilization attempts to sublimate emotions in the creation of a rationally ordered world.

Foucault described the *collection of rules* as that "which differentiates the permissible from the forbidden, natural from monstrous, normal from pathological, what is decent from what is not, and so on" (as cited in Rabinow, 1994, p. 200). This ordering of the world—the sense that it is possible to separate the "natural from the monstrous"—may only be imaginable through the lens of civilization. For our hunter-gatherer ancestors, who lived more intimately with the land and each other, such distinctions may have been inconceivable. The clan member one depended on for survival was also potentially the same person who could incite bloody competition. Likewise, nature could be abundant in the spring, but she could also be brutally withholding in the winter. Love, dependence, and power were inseparable; they required constant negotiation and a deep acceptance of ambivalence. Rather than a collection of rules ordering our ancestors' worlds, accepting this ambivalence and mastering the nuances of emotional communication would have brought order to their lives. Instead of arranging their lives for constancy—as distinctions between the normal and the pathological attempt to do—their world likely required an acceptance of the inevitability of change.

In the place of a collection of rules governing the creation of self, the principle of ambivalence likely organized our ancestors' construction of selfhood. Furthermore, in contrast to rules, myths and rituals showed the way through chaos and contradiction. As poet and anthropologist Stanley Diamond observed, "The principle of ambivalence is incorporated into the myths and rituals of primitive peoples to an extraordinary degree and a variety of ways" (1972, p. xii). In indigenous myths, the principle of ambivalence is witnessed through the antics of the Trickster. Paul Radin gave the following description of the Trickster:

> Trickster is at one and the same time creator and destroyer, giver and negator, he who dupes others and who is always duped himself. He wills nothing consciously. At all times he is constrained to behave as he does from impulses over which he has no control. He knows neither good nor evil yet he is responsible for both. He possesses no values, moral or social, is at the mercy of his passions and appetites, yet through his actions all values came into being. (1972, p. xxiii)

Radin's description of the Trickster reminds me of the often unpredictable and uncontrollable nature of emotions that the Enlightenment's conception of modern man, with its emphasis on the human capacity for reason, was designed to suppress. Diamond, however, saw this suppression occurring much earlier in human history, as far back as the birth of civilization. He noted that with the emergence of civilization, "the concrete image of the Trickster is suppressed, and simultaneously transformed into the problem of injustice" (1972, p. xiii).

Civilization coexists with the need to respond to injustices, and they may, in fact, emerge together. When people who once roamed freely began to interact—and *transact*—regularly in cities, injustice and the need for laws likely became a concern. For the first time, strangers became dependent on one another for their survival (Armstrong, 2001). They had to learn to trust in ways never needed during the millions of years their ancestors lived in loosely structured but close-knit groups in which everyone knew just about everything about everyone else—their flaws, their virtues, and their shifting alliances. In the cities, rules and regulations began to govern relationships that were once mediated principally through social-emotional bonds and shared associations.

A psychological tension is thought to have emerged with the shift to living in cities and nation-states. Civilizations maintain order through laws rather than the pursuit of emotional needs, so citizens suppress their innate social-emotional wisdom for civilization's abstract notions of fairness. For those who see civilization as an advancement over "primitive" life, suppression of emotions is thought to be a reasonable exchange for living as civilized peoples. The resulting internal tension is also seen as a natural development of the human psyche.

Sigmund Freud spoke of this tension as a fundamental aspect of human experience, reflecting the division of the human psyche into id, ego, and superego, in which neurosis and the need to repress instinct (the id) was the price of a civilized life (1930/1994). Similarly, Jung saw the Trickster as a primitive part of the human psyche: "It [the Trickster] holds the earlier low intellectual and moral level before the eyes of the more highly developed individual, so that he shall not forget how things looked yesterday" (1956/1972, p. 207). For both Freud and Jung, leaving behind the emotionally unpredictable aspects of human nature is not only a positive feature of civilization but also parallels the evolution of human psychological development.

These attitudes underscore the modern obsession with civilization and the idea that the growth of modern societies mirrors humans' psychological progress. Trickster, and the principle of ambivalence, becomes an emblem for the chaos and savagery civilization has supposedly enabled humankind to escape. Yet those who challenge the notion of civilization as superior to the hunter-gatherer and other indigenous ways of life instead cast the Trickster and our emotional drives as innately adaptive (Hyde, 1998; Pelton, 1989). Rather than solely a source of chaos or a threat to civilization, the Trickster is also valued as a representation of the transformative aspects of life, necessary for the evolution of both psyche and society. The Trickster figure in myth is the quintessential boundary breaker, whether through challenging taboos or defaming the sacred. Through the Trickster, societies stay alive by staying receptive to what is placed outside their boundaries. And through the practice of boundary breaking, old norms give way to new ways of being. Open discourse and social change are possible.

Robert Pelton described the Trickster as "the one who opens passageways into all that is still wild, and who transforms social boundaries into modes of intercourse" (1989, p. 236). I believe that the human need to challenge boundaries to begin new discourses and ways of being, mythologized through the Trickster, contributed to the evolution of dissociation as a psychological and social mechanism.

This is witnessed in Fabrega's characterization of trance and possession as forms of dissociation used to defend against the threat of social alienation and to communicate to others the need for social support. For example, when trance overcame someone, the shaman would bring together the entire clan to heal the ensuing "rape of the soul" (Levine, 1997, p. 57). With everyone present, there was a greater possibility for collective cohesion to be reestablished, and new discourses could emerge along with new social dynamics. Similarly, possession was an opportunity to articulate what otherwise would remain unspeakable. Through the supposed spirit's words, previously silenced travesties were brought to the community's attention.

Jung also made a connection between Trickster and dissociation when he described the Trickster as the *shadow* aspects of the self, stating, "It [the Trickster] is split off from his consciousness and consequently behaves like an autonomous personality" (1956/1972, p. 209). Similar to his discussion of the Trickster, Jung said of the relationship between trauma and dissociation: "A traumatic complex brings about the dissociation of the psyche. The complex is not under the control of the will and for this reason it possesses the quality of psychic autonomy" (as cited in Wilkinson, 2006, p. 95). However, I believe that because Jung saw Trickster as primarily a psychological remnant of an inferior human existence, he failed to see dissociation's potentially socially transformative power. In contrast, Pelton (1989) wrote:

> Because the Trickster pulls the most unyielding matter—disease, ugliness, greed, lust, lying, jealousy—into the orbit of life, and because especially in divination, he links these anomalies in their most commonplace forms to the taxonomies of communal life, he reveals how it is precisely on the plane of the daily and the specific that time is cooled down, social order enlarged, and all experience opened to transformation. (p. 252)

Rather than just a sign of psychic regression or defense, the mythical Trickster reveals how, through the acceptance of ambivalence, the possibility of transforming societies, relationships, and psyches always exists.

Similarly, dissociation does more than relieve unbearable psychic suffering; it also communicates to others that the social situation has become emotionally untenable. Just as certain facial expressions have universal meaning, I believe dissociation evolved to communicate the universal threat that alienation represents and anemic or nonexistent social-emotional bonds can cause. Dissociation may have also evolved as the veritable canary in the coal mine, a warning that social conditions are unsustainable due to overwhelming stress or social strain. Dissociation thus speaks to the need for transformation. It is a silent cry for social support and increased social-emotional bonds. Furthermore, I believe soul-making is pronounced when social-emotional bonds overcome dissociative defenses, enabling the traumatized person to regain trust in love and human connection. In the rest of this chapter, I share how the loss of the transformative power of dissociation in late modern America—and with it, the Trickster's principle of ambivalence—creates the conditions for dissociative defenses to become purely psychological phenomena, leaving many unconsciously defended against soul.

A Collection of Rules: Frozen Trust

Since the inception of the United States of America, the division between the public and private spheres of life was meant to protect individuals from exploitive, centralized power. The attention given to personal rights was initially a reaction to religious persecution and other forms of oppression many had endured in their homelands, including exploitation through unfair taxation and the threat of occupation. Though America's first citizens came from many different societies and held many different beliefs, they shared the traumatizing effects common to all people with histories of oppression and persecution.

When laws were first created to protect individual rights and balance power within the government, the image of the white male was epitomized as *the* individual whose rights were to be protected, whereas his wife, children, and slaves, as his property, were only protected via their association with him. Enlightenment philosophers such as René Descartes established that man was basically a rational being and at least theoretically capable of upholding laws and making reasonable choices about his own destiny. With the private sphere governed by reason, the public sphere could be devoted largely to supplying public works and protection from threats, supposedly the only support required for man's unrestrained fulfillment of his individual destiny.

However, as illustrated in Chapter Two, an alternative understanding of human nature is emerging that shows, rather than reason, the human capacity for creating social-emotional bonds is fundamental for the construction of selfhood. Furthermore, when these bonds are threatened or absent, dissociation is a likely response. We become fully actualized human beings through other people, not the protection of individual rights. Yet we are also, as de Waal asserted, a "Janus faced" species, "the product of opposing forces, such as the need to think of our own interests and the need to get along" (2005, pp. 220–221). Our American notion of democracy has left us largely unable to cope with unbridled quests for power that threaten our equally important need for social cohesion. As Borgmann observed, "Far from delimiting and clarifying individualism, the public-private distinction is itself an almost artfully complex confusion of where to locate authority and responsibility in the modern project" (1992, pp. 39–40).

America has attempted to make up for the lack of a robust public life by creating two social arenas where power and status displays are exercised: the capitalistic economy and the nuclear family. However, both suffer from the lack of the transformative forces the Trickster symbolized and are plagued by the unchecked pursuit of power. In the next two sections, I look at how power in these two arenas contributes to the need for dissociative defenses in our late modern society.

Capitalism in Our Global Age

The United States emerged during an era of unprecedented globalized activity and recently entered a new era of globalization. Similar to the prior globalization, which led to the establishment of the first American colonies, the current globalizing forces are also redistributing power and wealth. Countries such as Brazil, Russia, India, and China (the so-called *BRIC* nations) have become global competitors, increasing competition for jobs and commodities in a market once largely determined by Americans' voracious consumption of goods. Whereas increased competition is thought to have "flattened" the global hierarchy that once excluded many countries and individuals from reaping financial benefits, it also perpetuates old distinctions between the personal and private spheres of life that leave us ill-equipped to deal with the quest for power and status that is an inevitable aspect of humankind (Friedman, 2005). According to Borgmann, "We persist in designating a large part of the economy as private so we can disavow public responsibility for its evils and claim merit for its blessings" (1992, p. 43).

Early in American history, the unbridled pursuit of economic advancement became associated with the ideal of rugged individualism and the celebration of individual autonomy (Borgmann, 1992). The era of globalization that initiated such ideals emerged on the heels of the Industrial Revolution, with its increased dependency on natural resources and marketplaces to support a mercantile economy. Through sheer will, determination, and hard work, it was believed that anyone could become part of this ever-expanding capitalistic way of life. There was no sense that constraints needed to be placed on the resources exploited in the pursuit of power and status. Likewise, there was little regard for the psychological impact of the vast discrepancies in wealth—and power—that were emerging. Instead, the focus was on protecting the individual's right to manifest his own destiny. However, after nearly 250 years of manifesting destinies, rather than a nation of rational beings, we have become, as Frances Moore Lappé contended, "selfish little accumulators" (2004). Even the most basic necessity of life —water—has become a commodity.

One of the primary differences between the first era of globalization, which led to the formation of the United States, and our current era is that the unforeseen consequences of the capitalistic way of life have led to unanticipated risks. In our era of increased competition, limited resources, environmental degradation, and the resulting political instability, the once unbridled pursuit of power and status through material attainment has become overshadowed by uncertainty about the sustainability of the individualist way of life. According to cultural critic Gabe Mythen:

> Economic convergence, political fluctuation and national insecurity have become the motifs of the age. We are living in a "runaway" world" stippled by ominous dangers, military conflicts and environmental hazards. As a result, increasing portions of our everyday lives are spent negotiating change, dealing with uncertainty and assessing the personal impacts of situations that appear to be out of our control. In one way or another, the defining markers of modern society are all associated with the phenomenon of risk. (2004, p. 1)

It seems like the perfect time to revisit myths of the Trickster and re-engage with the transformative aspects of our basic human nature. As Pelton observed, "The Trickster only synthesizes because he first disrupts"—and it is hard to imagine a more disruptive social scene that the current global age (1989, p. 246).

Yet the conditions of late modern American society are not yet amenable to a complete break with the past. In large part, this is due to the continual perpetuation of the distinction between private and public spheres of life, which I believe currently inhibits meaningful social change. For social change to be meaningful requires social-emotional bonds to sustain a commitment to a new way of being.

Indeed, the presence of such bonds may be necessary for *any* experience to be meaningful. McFarlane and van der Kolk observed, "Emotional attachment is probably the primary protection against feelings of helplessness and meaninglessness; it is essential for biological survival in children, and without it, existential meaning is unthinkable in adults" (1996, p. 24).

As we collectively watch the destruction of environments and communities in the unending pursuit of status through material attainment, feelings of fear and helplessness have become widespread, along with an awareness of the meaninglessness of the clamor for more and more wealth (Gottschalk, 2000). Yet we less often observe how the vast majority of us continue to work and live as if the destruction of the planet is a foregone conclusion—as if we are unable to make the meaningful social changes necessary for survival.

The collection of rules we are expected to follow as rational subjects orders our late modern institutions and contributes to the sense of meaninglessness. Like the rationalist model of humans undergirding modernity, the institutions constructed to serve us suffer from a failure to grasp the fundamental nature and needs of human beings. Rather, as abstract systems, our institutions are characterized by the rules that govern them rather than the relationships that sustain them. Too often they are run by no one in particular—anyone with the appropriate specialized knowledge can ensure their proper execution—yet they require the complete trust of the people who depend on them for their functioning. Without this blind trust, abstract systems cannot work. How else could you hand over your money to a complete stranger—the "teller"—just because he stands behind the counter at your local bank? It is not the teller you trust but the rules and laws that supposedly protect your deposits.

Anthony Giddens contrasted the blind trust of modernity's

abstract systems with the trust that unfolds through social-emotional bonds:

> Traditional systems of trust were nearly always based on "facework". . . . [In contrast] the disembedded characteristics of abstract systems meant constant interaction with "absent others"—a person one never sees or meets but whose actions directly affect features of one's own life. (1994, p. 89)

In the example of the bank transaction, you have to assume the members of the Federal Reserve Bank are committed to upholding the laws governing deposits. In actuality, as Giddens argued, abstract systems like banks are at best "volatile mechanisms of trust" because they lack the social-emotional bonds and face-to-face communication that create more enduring trust—the kind of trust also necessary for meaningful social change (p. 90).

For abstract systems to function, their dependents must come to accept what Giddens referred to as *frozen trust*, which is expressed through the dependents' willingness to compulsively take part in the systems without the social-emotional bonds that over millions of years humans came to expect were part of any meaningful social relationship. According to Giddens, frozen trust "is commitment which has no object but is self-perpetuating"—and it has an addictive quality (1994, p. 90). In late modern America, we are overrun with the need to compulsively engage with frozen trust in our attempts to secure a place in society. This compulsivity is witnessed in the unending quest for wealth. Not unlike an addiction, the compulsive pursuit of wealth is an illusionary grasping that replaces what was once one of the more meaningful aspects of community: the opportunity to create real trust through social-emotional bonds that contribute to meaningful, emotionally bonding alliances.

In late modern American society, manifesting one's destiny

rarely has the transformative power fantasized through images of the rugged individual who once positively portrayed earlier grabs for wealth. Unrestrained by adequate checks and balances—lacking the ridicule and humiliation that kept members of egalitarian societies from pitting their interests above others—late modern American society insufficiently regulates pursuits of power and status, leading to a profoundly inequitable society. For example, from 1990 to 2005, CEO compensation increased by almost 300%, while production workers' wages remained almost stagnant, gaining only 4.3% (Domhoff, 2005). Furthermore, America has the greatest income disparity of all Westernized nations: 1% of the population controls 40% of all the wealth (Sapolsky, 2005).

In the latest round of globalization, America has emerged with a corporatist model of government committed more to the country's financial success and protection from external threats than the democratic share of power at home. Journalist Naomi Klein, in her book *The Shock Doctrine* (2007), characterized the emerging corporatist model of government as "huge transfers of public wealth to private hands, often accompanied by exploding debt, an ever-widening chasm between the dazzling rich and the disposable poor and an aggressive nationalism that justifies bottomless spending on security" (p. 15). Signs of this emerging corporatist government in late modern America include soaring dept, continual involvement in foreign conflicts, the highest incarceration rate in the world, the deterioration of social services, and a widening gap between rich and poor (Chaddock, 2003).

In our globalized information age, increased opportunity to buy things has also come with an increased awareness of what others have. No longer do we look only to friends, neighbors, and coworkers to gauge our efforts at garnering status. Through the internet we can become intimately familiar with the lives of exceedingly wealthy people and their extraordinary and unimaginable lifestyles. Indeed, today it has become common-place to know more about the lives of celebrities than one's next-door neighbor. Giddens pointed out:

> Instantaneous electronic communication isn't just a way in which news or information is conveyed more quickly. Its existence alters the very texture of our lives, rich and poor alike. When the image of Nelson Mandela maybe is more familiar to us than the face of our next door neighbour, something has changed in the nature of everyday experience. (1999)

Lacking the social checks and balances of a smaller egalitarian society, we are caught in a race for the biggest/best/latest commodities and the most impressive lifestyles. And this commodity race is making us sick. Researchers at the University of California, San Francisco, discovered that our perceived socioeconomic status is as good a predictor of cardiovascular disease, obesity, and levels of stress hormones as our actual socioeconomic status (Singh-Manoux et al., 2003). Thus, *feeling* poor is as bad for your health as actually *being* poor. And countries like America, with the highest levels of economic inequality, were the most likely to support these results.

As noted earlier, the effects of trauma-related stress correlate with many health problems (Felitti et al., 1998). The same diseases associated with status-related stress are also associated with a history of adverse childhood experiences. This is likely more than a coincidence. In both situations, the individual experiences a sense of inescapability from circumstances, which contributes to the stress experienced—and, I would argue, the need for dissociative defenses to cope. Furthermore, according to biologist Robert Sapolsky, the most important contributors to reducing stress occur through relationships with others, and hence, the creation of social-emotional bonds (2005).

Although the medical model is responsible for uncovering the relationship between status and health, it has not been forthcoming with ways to challenge the social inequalities that contribute to disease. Medical care is also one of the abstract systems that rely on frozen trust, despite the interpersonal dynamics on which it depends.

Advances in molecular biology initiated a turn away from the social environment to the person's physiology as the source of disease, including mental disorders. The shift to the body as the origin of mental illness made it possible to speak of mental disorders as determined by the structure of the living being. Canguilhem associated this conceptual shift with the introduction of the phrase *hereditary biochemical error*—what we today refer to as genetic disorders. With the term "error," Canguilhem stated, "a new nomenclature of disease is thus established, referring disease not to the individual considered in its totality but to its morphological and functional constituents" (1977/1998, p. 140).

One consequence is that the contextually bounded meanings found in cultures and societies are suppressed by molecular biology's conceptions of the normal and the abnormal— much as civilization's collection of rules suppresses the Trickster principle of ambivalence. Social-emotional bonds are simply cut out of the process, and along with them the possibility of transformative change that might lead to less dependency on dissociative defenses for survival. Biomedical psychiatry also supports a depersonalized approach to relationships in general, a dissociative stance that psychiatrist R. D. Laing described as a normal trait in the modern world:

A partial depersonalization of others is extensively practised in everyday life and is regarded as normal if not highly desirable. Most relationships are based on some partial depersonalizing tendency in so far as one treats the other not in terms of any awareness of who or what he might be in himself but as virtually an android robot playing a role or part in a large machine in which one too may be acting yet another part. (1969, p. 47)

Similarly, Jung claimed, "If for 'person' we substitute 'modern society,' it is evident that the latter is suffering from a mental dissociation" (as cited in Storr, 1957/1983, p. 384).

Biomedical psychiatrists often bypass opportunities for creating social-emotional bonds in their interactions with patients. They regularly neglect personal narratives of suffering as they listen for the biological origin of disease. In her ethnographic study of psychiatry residency programs, T. M. Luhrmann described how Nick, a psychiatrist, filtered his patient's narrative of suffering, searching for the rhythms of her brain (2001). Nick "wanted to learn, by listening to her [the patient] and asking her questions, whether she was concentrating better, whether she was feeling more energetic or more depressed, and when, and what kind of energy or anxiety or depression it felt like" (p. 135). Luhrmann portrayed psychiatrist and patient as inhabiting different worlds of meaning: "The patient was telling the doctor about her soul's history, and he was hearing through it the shape and balance of her brain" (p. 135).

The sociologist David Karp's first experience with a psychiatrist was similar:

I assumed that I would once again be asked to give the shortened version of my biography. I was surprised, therefore, to learn that Dr. Rosen was not at all interested in my relationships with my parents, my siblings, my wife, my children, or my job. He simply asked a series of questions about my symptoms. Did it feel the worst in the morning? Did I feel an elevation in mood in mid-afternoon? Did I fall asleep quickly only to wake an hour later? Did I often finally fall asleep between 5:30 and 7 in the morning? And so on. (1996, p. 8)

To be a good patient—to take responsibility for his disease —Karp learned to identify his symptoms, note the effects of his medications, and notify his doctor of any changes that would suggest the presence of disease. Unlike the shaman, who brings the community together to return the soul to the body, the biomedical psychiatrist completely bypasses the social context of suffering—and teaches the patient to do so as well— avoiding the potentially transformative power of dissociative defenses that Fabrega argued may be precursors to all mental disorders.

The Trickster is absent, too, in the biomedical encounter. The Trickster, as rule breaker, forever challenges social norms, confusing the sacred with the profane and the normal with the pathological, thereby keeping the possibility of social transfor- mation alive. Pelton stated, "The Trickster reveals the elasticity of those boundaries; or better, reveals that they are membranes through which life passes into the future and death, and at the same time flows back again to its beginnings and new life" (1989, p. 240). Yet biomedical psychiatry and other abstract systems want nothing of the Trickster and his anarchic ways, so the Trickster is summarily dismissed before the boundary- breaking pranks can ever commence. Instead of Trickster boundary breaking, psychiatry witnesses the incoherent words of psychosis. By virtue of being pathologized, these potentially boundary-breaking discourses are ignored. The language of madness is suppressed by the language of symptoms that parcel self-expression into evidence of disorder, silencing souls and potential avenues for social transformation.

Power and the Family

Frozen trust has also infiltrated the private sphere in America, initially epitomized by the nuclear family. However, the nuclear family is more fantasy than reality in late modern America. In 2000, less than 25% of the households in America were made up of married couples and their children (Schmitt, 2001). Increasingly, families are headed by a single mother and are often a lot poorer than two-parent households, potentially increasing the impact of status-stress on its members. Blended families and unmarried couples raising children are also increasingly the norm.

However, changes in family structures and dynamics have not alleviated the pressures placed on this protected private space. On the contrary, the American home has become an outlet for the power inequities left unaddressed in the public sphere—and it is often a very violent space. As sociologist Zygmunt Bauman observed, "An admixture of violence is now suspected and expected to appear in the most intimate relationships, where love and mutual well-wishing were supposed to rule supreme" (1995, p. 156).

Today we know the family is where the tensions associated with unfair power differentials in the public arena are absorbed. Addictions, domestic violence, and childhood abuse have all been identified as predominant conditions in American homes today. They are also associated with feelings of powerlessness in the larger public sphere (Butler, 1996; Chesler, 1989; Herman, 1997), as well as traumatic stress, stress-related diseases, mental disorders, and suicide (Chapmana et al., 2004; Felitti et al., 1998; Lyons-Ruth et al., 2006). In her interviews with male perpetrators of incest, Sandra Butler repeatedly witnessed how feelings of powerlessness in the public arena led to dominance displays in the home. "When some men feel themselves to be powerless in the outside world, they become, while they are in their homes, utterly despotic" (1996, p. 73). Psychologist Judith Herman observed more generally, "Psychological trauma is an affliction of the powerless" (1997, p. 33).

Because America is devised to protect the private sphere from external threats, it has unwittingly created the very conditions in which traumatic defenses such as dissociation become necessary for survival. Herman pointed out that isolation is one of the key components associated with family violence: "It is by now a common place that families in which child abuse occurs are socially isolated" (1997, p. 100). The intense fear, helplessness, loss of control, and threat of annihilation that are common feelings of being terrorized in the isolated home are the conditions that contribute to traumatic defenses like dissociation (Herman, 1997). The isolation experienced by children in violent and chaotic households becomes internalized as well, as they learn not to trust relationships or love.

The lack of social trust that is a common outcome of adverse childhood experiences may contribute to the likelihood of investing in frozen trust and the pursuit of status in the public sphere. Social-emotional bonds become perceived as risky and potentially threatening. For many, it may seem safer to invest in a rational worldview that does not challenge the dissociative defenses previously necessary for surviving violence and emotional alienation in the home. Levine believed:

> Disconnection from our felt sense of belonging leaves our emotions foundering in a vacuum of loneliness. It leaves our rational minds to create fantasies based on disconnection rather than connection. These fantasies compel us to compete, make war, distrust one another, and undermine our natural respect for life. If we do not sense our connection with all things, then it is easier to destroy or ignore these things. Human beings are naturally cooperative and loving.

We enjoy working together. However, without fully integrated brains, we cannot know this about ourselves. (1997, p. 266).

Imagining Beyond Dissociation

It may be through the imaginal aspects of the psyche that we are most likely to break the divide between public and private arenas and reclaim the transformative space necessary for letting go of dissociative defenses. In fact, it may not be merely serendipitous that one of the most defining features of the late modern landscape is its saturation with imagery through television, the internet, ubiquitous advertising, and music. The late modern landscape constitutes what sociologist Simon Gottschalk described as a "mediated world" (2000). In media we find the Trickster most at play, challenging divisions between the sacred and profane and, I imagine, pushing for opportunities to break through the fragmentation and power abuses dominating the late modern American landscape. Gottschalk observed:

> We are in turn bombarded by pictures not only of hopelessly unattainable images of idealized identities, but also images of past and present suffering, images of destruction, of bodies quite literally in pieces. We are ourselves "torn" in the process, not only emotionally and morally but in the fragmentary structure of the act of looking itself. In an image-saturated environment which increasingly resembles the interior space of subjective fantasy turned inside out, the very subject-object distinction begins to break down, and the subject comes apart in the space of its own making. (p. 28)

However, rather than transforming, the mediated, imaginal world of late modernity perpetuates dissociative defenses and fantasy in which excess subjectivity and a wall of alienation are increasingly becoming normative. Without trust in love or opportunities for social-emotional bonds to transform defenses, many Americans are increasingly defended not only against connections with one another but their own possibilities for soul-making.

The capitalistic system that has turned American democracy into a predominantly corporatist society promotes the compulsive pursuit of power and status, creating intense social stress as the country becomes strained by unsustainable differences in wealth. Some of our institutions, like medicine, teach us how to ignore our own stories and cries for help. Medicine shows us how to articulate their abstract rules for disease, identifying the normal and the pathological in ourselves, in effect redoubling dissociative defenses against the overwhelming stress and heartache that often lead to medical intervention in the first place.

In our intimate relationships, we are often hurt the most and learn to dissociate as a defense against overwhelming and often traumatic stress. Indeed, as shared in Chapter Two, it is through the infant-caregiver bond that the developing child first learns to dissociate as a defense against the threat of emotional alienation (Lyons-Ruth et al., 2006). Yet due to bonds with caregivers, we are also likely to first experience empathy, love, and the tending of our souls. Thus, it is likely through intimate relationships that we will find opportunities to move out of late modern stagnation. As Giddens remarked:

> The post-traditional society is an ending; but it is also a beginning, a genuinely new social universe of action and experience. What type of social order is it, or might it become? . . . It is one where social bonds have effectively to be made (1994, p. 107).

How will these bonds be made? According to Giddens,

"Talk, or dialogue, are the basis of making the relationship work" (1999). I agree with Giddens; communication is an essential component of well-functioning relationships. However, what and how we communicate are relevant to overcoming dissociative defenses against the creation of soul. For millions of years, we have adapted for *emotional* communication, and dissociation emerges in response to the failure to sustain social-emotional bonds. To prevent dissociation from defending against soul-making, we must speak the language of the soul, which is both emotional and imaginal. Carl Jung wrote about his exploration of the imaginal: "To the extent that I managed to translate the emotions into images—that is to say, to find the images which were concealed in the emotions—I was inwardly calmed and reassured" (1989, p. 177). I believe the soul is tended when this connection between the imaginal and emotions is made through our relationships with others.

Like Jung before them, imaginal psychologists believe the psyche created through soul-making is inherently imaginative. Hillman remarked, "Everything we know and feel and every statement we make are fantasy-based" (1975, p. xvii). To say all experiences are "fantasy-based" highlights the centrality of the imagination for creating soul, in which fantasy includes both day and night dreams, reflective speculations, and images. All psychic experiences—both conscious and unconscious—are enlivened by the imagination.

This conception of the soul as fundamentally imaginal contradicts the dominant modern understanding of the human psyche, which favors egoistic, conscious experiences and rational thought. Hillman depicted modern psychology as "engaged in ego-making and not soul-making" (1975, p. 48). Imaginal psychology attempts to revise modern psychology, returning the soul and imagination to their rightful place in psychic experience. Imaginal psychology challenges the narrow description of the human psyche as ego driven. It rejects the dominant belief that we discover truths about the world through rationality and consciousness, while the imaginal and the unconscious contribute to delusions and mental illness. Rather than pathologizing imaginal experiences, imaginal psychology witnesses the *telos* of the symptom. Instead of looking for pathology, it is concerned with *pathos* and the drive to create meaning through suffering.

The imaginal is archetypal, reconnecting us to our hunter-gatherer ancestors for whom the nature of human experience was expressed through mythological motifs, including the Trickster as a representation of the role of ambivalence for transformation. Rather than objectifying the world and identifying truths, as ego-driven psychologies attempt to do, our ancestors' myths reflected a way of *being* in the world. Thoughts, emotions, and imagery were inseparable, defying measurement and control. Instead, they were personified through mythical motifs. The result was the language of the soul and a way to perceive and sense the world and make sense of emotions—and in the process personify both self and the world. Hillman remarked, "To enter myth we must personify; to personify carries us into myth" (1975, p. 16).

Poet and religious scholar Roberts Avens accurately depicted imaginal psychology as "a struggle for a wholly new (yet most ancient and religious) experience of reality" (1980, p. 40). Imaginal psychology returns us to the hunter-gatherer psyche. Through imaginal psychology, we witness once again the centrality of soul-making for the human psyche, its expression through the imaginal, and the personification of the psyche, through which we populate our inner worlds. Through soul-making, we cross the divide between self and other, finding the outer world in ourselves and the inner world played out in reality. Through the imaginal we keep these worlds lively, meaningful, and in play.

The poet, playwright, and novelist Miguel de Unamuno

once said, "In order to love everything, in order to pity every-thing, human and extra-human, living and non-living, you must feel everything within yourself, you must personalize everything" (as cited in Hillman, 1975, p. 15). I believe that we come to personalize the world through the relationship between the imaginal and emotional. I also agree with Avens that "images are the only reality we apprehend directly" (1980, p. 34). I hypothesize that when images bridge the intermediary space of soul, they also lessen the distance between self and other.

Through the imaginal, not only do we create soul, but we also bring the world into us, giving meaning to feelings and avoiding dissociative defenses that would otherwise protect a solitary self that has evolved for living with close emotional connections to others. We have souls because we are connected with others. Perhaps this is why Chodorow (1997) asserted, "Fantasy must be allowed the freest possible play, yet not in such a manner that it leaves the orbit of its object, namely the affect" (p. 7). If we assume that human survival depended on developing a sufficient emotional repertoire to sustain connec-tion, would not the imaginal—as the meaning maker and soul maker—become meaningless when it lost its ability to connect us to what we feel and to others?

Psychotherapist Andrew Samuels (1985) asserted, "Images must be experienced, caressed, played with, reversed, responded to—in short, related to (felt) rather than solely inter-preted or explained (thought)" (p. 242). I believe he is correct, although his emphasis is misplaced. Living in the shadow of the Enlightenment's elevated sense of the value of reason, it is important to dismantle the rational perspective of human nature that thwarts the natural tendency to feel the world through imagery. However, by focusing energies against modernism's obsession with consciousness and rational thought, Samuels risks missing how the imaginal deepens soul

through our opportunities to *feel with others*. The Enlightenment not only lost the imaginal but also community. I believe
humans have soul only because emotions and the imaginal
create a yearning to go beyond the limits of what the body can
sense. Through the imaginal, we escape our aloneness and live
internally and externally in the company of others. We become,
as James Hollis observed, "all part of one psychic family" (2000,
p. 19).

I experienced how the imaginal contributes to both soul
and human connection when sharing a memory from childhood with my Pacifica classmate John. I told him the story of
my first crush in grade school on an African American boy.
Although my parents were amused, they told me to keep my
new relationship secret from my grandparents, who would
disapprove of my affections for a boy with dark skin. It was my
earliest recollection of racism and learning to be for others to
feel loved. This was a lesson I would learn continuously
throughout my life and one that I challenge as part of my indi-
viduation process. It has been painful to lose so many aspects
of myself in the vain hope of receiving the love that was often
absent in my childhood.

When I shared my memory with John, his face showed
empathy for the little girl who just wanted to love and be loved.
He pointed to two trees near where we were sitting on the
sunny lawn outside the classroom and gave me two images: one
was of the natural tree, whose branches curled every which
way and stood majestically in its uniqueness; the other was the
topiary, the tree pruned to fit the whims of another. His images
stunned me, and my soul drank them up. They were the perfect
expression of what I felt had occurred in my family of origin
and my relationship with myself. However, those images do not
exist disembodied in my mind. Rather, they are held with the
image of John and his kindness, expressed through the giving
of the images to me. The images are forever connected with the

feeling of being understood by another, and as such, they validate me and deepen me, nourishing my soul in the process.

I believe the power of the imaginal lies not only in the image but also in the gift of imagery. The images that reveal to us ourselves, as well as the images we hope to grow into, are attached to emotions, and emotions are what connect us to others. The relationship is not a causal one; rather, it is simultaneous, multiple, playful, and deeply personifying. I would venture that every image that deepens soul is in some way attached to another person or something personified. Herein lies the power I perceive in the imaginal for healing dissociation and returning to soul: it is our natural way to populate the psyche with others, desperately needed in a world that is increasingly alienating.

Late modern American society is not lacking in the imaginal nor opportunities to share imagery. On the contrary, we are overrun with imagery. Just in terms of commercial advertisements, the average American is exposed to over three thousand messages a day (Shenk, 1997). But the imaginal saturating the late modern world seems more part of the compulsiveness that perpetuates the frozen trust of late modernity than a practice of soul-making. In the next section, I conclude with Donald Kalsched's (1996) self-care system to describe how dissociation contributes to the fantasy-based world in which we live and is increasingly becoming a defense against soul.

Dissociation as Self-Care

In his book *The Inner World of Trauma*, Donald Kalsched described an archetypal defense system activated by childhood trauma (1996). Once in place, it becomes an entrenched psychological defense mechanism, which Jung referred to as *dissociation* and Kalsched associated with the Trickster and personified as the daimon: "Our daimon *appears to personify the psyche's dissociative defenses in those cases where early trauma has made psychic integration impossible*" (p. 11). The daimon becomes the basis of an elaborate fantasy world that emerges to protect the fragile psyche from real-world threats. Both benevolently loving and malevolently cruel, the daimon's purpose is unwavering: protecting an underdeveloped aspect of the psyche from further harm.

One of the outcomes of the self-care system is a schizoid state in which fantasy becomes a defense against engaging meaningfully with reality. The normal developmental process that leads to healthy attachment with real people is thwarted by early life trauma, whether from childhood abuse, emotional neglect, or other adverse experiences. Instead, the sense of the "I" and the "other" are enclosed within the self through fantasy without the necessary investment in real-world relationships that would lead to both healthy interpersonal dynamics and a well-integrated psyche. As a result, the person dependent on the self-care system (and dissociative defenses) needs opportunities to learn to trust real relationships so they can let go of the need for the internal daimon protector.

The daimon serves as the internalized other and creates an inner world of fantasy that replaces real relationships. Concerning the daimon, Kalsched said: "By thus imprisoning a relatively 'innocent' part of the personality, it seeks to assure its protection from further abuse" (1996, p. 28). Sometimes imprisonment comes from a harsh, punitive internal critic that denigrates the innocent part so much that feeling worthy of love from others becomes unthinkable. Other times, the Trickster qualities dominate, distracting through addictions and other destructive behaviors that help maintain the self-care defense system as an integral part of psychic functioning. Kalsched remarked, "He [the daimon] becomes the inner voice that tempts the ego with intoxicating substances, including food or alcohol, away from any struggle with outer reality" (p. 28).

Although the self-care system can cause severe emotional suffering, particularly when it takes the form of a harsh, critical daimonic presence, it nevertheless buffers against the possibility of being hurt again in a real relationship. For the person with a childhood history of trauma, being psychologically imprisoned by a daimonic spirit is safer than risking loving a real person. Not surprisingly, overcoming the need for a self-care system requires a profound sense of safety, especially in the therapeutic relationship. The self-care system is constantly scanning for evidence that the real world is unsafe, and any verification of this belief justifies interventions by the daimon.

Earlier I shared results from the Adverse Childhood Experiences Study that revealed as many as two-thirds of Americans endured adverse conditions in childhood, many of which arguably could lead to the activation of the self-care system (Anda et al., 2004). Furthermore, addictions to substances and processes (including the compulsive pursuit of status) are an enormous problem in America and across the world. The media-drenched landscape we inhabit seems, at times, to serve internal fantasies and escape from reality generated through daimonic self-care systems that keep many of us unable to connect meaningfully with the outer world and one another.

Release from the self-care system requires an externalization of its repeated internal traumas. As Kalsched observed, "The unconscious repetition of traumatization in the inner world which goes on incessantly must become a real traumatization with an object in the world if the inner system is to be 'unlocked'" (1996, p. 26). Here we see the need for the other aspect of the Trickster witnessed in his transformative powers. Whereas he distracts and torments under the guise of self-defense, the Trickster also signifies the need for the external world to "break through" and reform the inner world of experience. Cultures such as the Yoruba, Fon, and Dogon saw the Trickster as a transformer because he "continually provokes intercourse between what is outside man and what is inside him" (Pelton, 1989, p. 234). This transformative power of the Trickster is lost through abstract laws and suppression of emotional ambivalence, which America upholds with its sharp distinctions between public and private spheres of life.

We need each other to break through our dissociative defenses—becoming the external "traumas" that bring forth the grief for what we have collectively lost through millennia of ignoring our deeply human need for social-emotional bonds. However, caught in the fantasies of our self-care systems, "we suffer for the want of that vanished world, a deep grief we learn to misconstrue" (Shepard, 1982, p. 15).

Summary

In this chapter, I completed my archaeology of emotions in late modern American society by looking at the emotional equivalent to Foucault's collection of rules: the principle of emotional ambivalence personified through the mythical Trickster. I showed how the Trickster's transformative power is suppressed through America's sharp distinctions between public and private arenas and the lack of opportunities for dissociation to be transformed through social-emotional bonds. Dominant conceptions of capitalism and the family contribute to unrestrained quests for power and increased feelings of alienation. In our isolation, many of us have become dissociatively defended against soul. The imaginal, which historically is the basis for emerging with soul, is more often fodder for fantasy-driven self-care systems that defend against the social-emotional connections necessary for tending the soul and overcoming dissociation.

4

CONCLUSION

It is true there is no resolution, only tragedy and a warning, in this African tale. But the woman who walked into the bloodred sunset of Africa to vanish, the servant in rags and tatters still haunting the corridors of my own mind, the woman abandoned and weeping in the ruined castle in the dream of the Spaniard, and indeed the naked, demented Bushman woman whimpering in the summer sunlight of the desert, each in her own way seemed to serve a single meaning. They all drew attention to the denial of something vital in the human spirit.

— Laurens van der Post, *The Heart of the Hunter*

I have attempted to construct an archaeology of emotions to understand how and why dissociation has become a dominant psychological and sociological defense in late modern America —if not large swaths of the world—transformed by the conditions of late modernity. The idea of creating an archaeology of emotions emerged from an earlier project in which I used

Michel Foucault's archaeology of thought to explore how people use the medical model of mental disorders to distance themselves from psychological suffering, create order in their lives, and give meaning to their existences (2000). At the time, I did not identify being diagnosed with a mental disorder as the loss of soul. Now I do. I also see the biomedical approach perpetuating the frozen trust and dissociative defenses that I associated in Chapter Three with institutions derived from Enlightenment ideology.

Throughout this project, I highlighted an emerging field of knowledge that identifies social-emotional bonds as a defining attribute of humankind. I also described the interdependency existing between social-emotional bonds and the soul, and I have looked at how intimate relationships and social conditions contribute to the predominance of dissociation in late modern America. My guiding hypothesis has been that the societal conditions of late modern America in particular and civilization in general are not amenable to humans' innate social and emotional needs, which have evolved over millions of years.

Instead, by promoting Enlightenment ideas that cast "man" as a rational being, American democracy has unwittingly led to a country lacking sufficient opportunities for people to foster the social-emotional bonds that are foundational for the creation of soul. America's sharp distinctions between public and private social arenas—and its failure to create opportunities for moderating quests for power that are a natural aspect of human societies—allows dissociation to become widespread and, at times, reach psychopathological proportions.

In our ancestors' hunter-gatherer societies, dissociation likely functioned as a psychological defense and a sign to others of the need for social-emotional bonds when the sufferer became too alienated. However, late modern America has become an increasingly alienating place. Livelihoods have become inexorably tied to the financial success of large corporations. A sizeable part of the population is expected to continuously reeducate, relocate, and reinvent themselves to stay active in the marketplace. The world, like the families many of us come from, is a risky place. The sheer amount of uncertainty makes it exceedingly difficult for many of us to experience lasting trust in anything, let alone each other. The norm is at risk of becoming, as Kalsched described, for our minds to be dominated by daimonic self-care systems that keep us locked safely away in our personal fantasy worlds, defended against the relationships that could release us from this dissociated state. The media-saturated world in which we live provides much material for escapist fantasies, which perhaps in a healthier world could be sources for imaginal sharing that deepens the soul. The saddest thing for me about this late modern state of affairs is that many of us are so completely defended against deep grief for the loss of our ancestors' world that we cannot even witness our need to mourn.

Implications of Dissociation as a Defense Against Soul

Two implications of dissociation being a defense against soul in late modern America came to mind while writing this thesis. First, once societal conditions are identified that contribute to the perpetuation of dissociative defenses, responding to dissociation becomes more than just the purview of the mental health system. On the contrary, responding to dissociation will likely require reforming society to meet our innate need for social-emotional bonds in ways that sustain emotional well-being and help regulate the quest for power and status. I believe this is vital for reducing the absurdly large number of people in America who endure adverse experiences in childhood (and later mental disorders), which often instill the need for dissociative defenses. Since dissociation is typically learned by the developing infant in relationship with their primary caregiver, greater resources for families and distressed caregivers are needed. We also need to rethink the safeguards that protect unbridled capitalism but that, perhaps, jeopardize the futures of our most vulnerable—and powerless—members of society.

Second, the ideas and research I have shared support devoting resources and energy to creating conditions in which dissociative defenses are witnessed and interpreted as a need for increased social-emotional bonds. For too long America has practiced medicalizing suffering, identifying collective problems as individual psychopathologies. Efforts need to be directed towards telling different stories about psychic suffering that not only include society as part of the problem but also identify altering the social milieu as part of the solution to reducing both dissociative defenses and mental disorders. Without such efforts I doubt we can save the planet from our destructive quest for status through material attainment, which, I believe, is the inevitable outcome of a majority of people psychically lost in fantasy-driven self-care defense systems.

Contributions to Depth Psychology

Depth psychotherapists have a unique opportunity to nurture not only the souls of their clients but also *anima mundi*, the collective spirit of the world. I have attempted to show why our fundamental need for emotional connection must be integrated into society's organization and institutions. However, by making a connection between personal and collective problems, I also hoped to imply the potential impact depth psychotherapists can have when they work with a client to reconnect with soul. Indeed, by nurturing the individual, we also nourish society.

I also highlighted the centrality of the imaginal for soul tending, which applies to psychotherapy. As a society we have become obsessed with the pursuit of the latest "tool" to release us from suffering, whether a pill, diagnosis, or treatment modality. The outcome of our sometimes-crazed attempts to escape suffering is that we are not creating the time, opportunity, or conditions needed for the inevitable mourning that follows centuries of human suffering caused by living in societies ill-adapted to our innate social and emotional needs. Perhaps by slowing down and making space for the imaginal to transform us, we can also thaw the deep grief frozen inside so many of us today.

Collectively, we have lost our way in the world. Even if we wanted to stop the current capitalistic way of life, we would still have to deal with all the degradation, disease, and destruction that overruns so much of the late modern world. Yet through the imaginal and making time for deep social-emotional bonds, we can nurture soul, personifying self, other, and world in the process—reviving the archetypal aspects of ourselves that we unconsciously yearn for—while mourning all that has been lost. Psychotherapists can resuscitate the archetypal and mythical ways of our early ancestors by paying attention to the imaginal, honoring its significance, and enlivening our clients' souls through loving attention to its presence. I believe the psychotherapeutic encounter is perhaps one of the few places in our society that is naturally amenable to doing this invaluable work, especially when a depth psychological approach informs the relationship between psychotherapist and client.

Suggestions for Further Exploration

When dissociation is understood as a sign of the need for social change, the creative aspects of psychic suffering can also be witnessed. Fabrega spoke of the creative aspects of dissociation. He believed dissociation may have been the precursor to the psychological development of modern humans. Through dissociation and the fantasy-driven self-care system, humans have taken the social world into themselves, fantasizing possibilities not actualized in the outer realm. Although this is a deeply personal process, it also is instigated through social conditions, especially situations that provoke pride, shame, and guilt (Turner, 2000).

Thus, although late modern America is overrun with dissociatively defended people, some of whom are identified as having a mental disorder, in the right conditions, these same people may be the ones who find creative solutions to the destructive conditions of the late modern world. Honoring dissociation's creative aspects would likely mean listening to madness rather than medicating it away, along with creating opportunities for meaningful inclusion in the community for some of our most troubled and powerless members. Much research is needed to design a mental health system and society that foster dissociation's innately creative potential and opportunities for regaining trust in love. To revolutionize, however, the research must be done with soul in mind.

Lasting Thoughts

As Fabrega contended, dissociation can contribute to imagining possibilities and protect against hurt. Through dissociation, we imagine worlds inside us to avoid the sense of alienation we feel in the outer world. And in the right conditions, dissociation can contribute to new ideas and ways of being in the world, signaling to others our readiness to return to the tribe. It is a Trickster dance, and writing embodies the process. Whereas real-world interactions provide the motivation and impetus to write, the act of writing requires splitting off from the world, creating an alienated state of the writer's own making. Yet the world writers anticipate returning to, with pages in hand, profoundly influences the quality of the work, including whether or not the work has soul. Thus, I end this project with the hope that my soulful longing will be heard and that this wounded researcher will be witnessed.

REFERENCES

American Psychiatric Association. (2008). *Diagnostic and statistical manual of mental disorders* (4th ed., text revision). Washington, DC: Author.

Anda, R. F., Fleisher, V. I., Felitti, V. J., Edwards, V. J., Whitfield, C. L., Dube, S. R., Williamson, David F. (2004). Childhood abuse, household dysfunction, and indicators of impaired adult worker performance. *The Permanente Journal, 8*(1), 30–38.

Andrews, P. (1996). Palaeoecology and hominoid palaeoenvironments. *Biological Review, 71,* 257–300.

Armstrong, K. (2001). *Buddha*. New York: Penguin.

Avens, R. (1980). Imagination in Jung and Hillman. In *Imagination is reality* (pp. 31–47). Dallas: Spring.

Bauman, Z. (1995). *Life in fragments*. Oxford: Basil Blackwell.

Beck, U. (1999). *World risk society*. Malden, MA: Blackwell.

Beck, U., Bonss, W., & Lau, C. (2003). The theory of reflexive modernization: Problematic, hypotheses and research programme. *Theory, Culture & Society, 20*(2), 1–33.

Begley, S. (2007, March 19). Beyond stones & bones. *Newsweek,* 52–58.

Borgmann, A. (1992). *Crossing the postmodern divide.* Chicago: University of Chicago Press.

Bowlby, J. (1973). *Attachment and loss: Volume 2, separation.* New York: Basic.

Burstow, B. (2003). Toward a radical understanding of trauma and trauma work. *Violence Against Women, 9*(11), 1293–1317.

Butler, S. (1996). *Conspiracy of silence: The trauma of incest.* Volcano, CA: Volcano Press.

Canguilhem, G. (1988). *Ideology and rationality in the history of the life sciences* (A. Goldhammer, Trans.). Cambridge, MA: MIT Press. (Original work published 1977)

Canguilhem, G. (1991). *The normal and the pathological* (C. R. Fawcett & R. S. Cohen, Trans.) (2nd ed.). New York: Zone Books. (Original work published 1966)

Carroll, S. B. (2006). *The making of the fittest: DNA and the ultimate forensic record of evolution.* New York: W. W. Norton.

Chaddock, G. R. (2003, August 18). US notches world's highest incarceration rate. *The Christian Science Monitor.* Retrieved April 5, 2010, from http://www.csmonitor.com/2003/0818/po2so1-usju.html.

Chapmana, D. P., Whitfield, C. L., Felitti, V. J., Dube, S. R., Edwards, V. J., & Anda, R. F. (2004). Adverse childhood experiences and the risk of depressive disorders in adulthood. *Journal of Affective Disorders, 82*, 217–225.

Chesler, P. (1989). *Women and madness.* New York: A Harvest/HBJ Book.

Chodorow, J. (1997). Introduction. In J. Chodorow (Ed.), *Jung on active imagination* (pp. 1–20). Princeton, NJ: Princeton University Press.

Clippinger, J. H. (2007). *A crowd of one: The future of individual identity.* New York: Public Affairs.

Cozolino, L. (2006). *The neuroscience of human relationships: Attachment and the developing brain.* New York: W. W. Norton.

De Waal, F. (2005). *Our inner ape: A leading primatologist explains why we are who we are.* New York: Riverhead.

Diamond, S. (1972). Introductory essay: Job and the Trickster. In P. Radin (Ed.), *The Trickster: A study in American Indian mythology* (pp. xi–xxii). New York: Schocken.

Domhoff, G. W. (2005, December 2006). Wealth, income, power. Retrieved November 27, 2007, from http://sociology.ucsc.edu/whorulesamerica/power/wealth.html.

Dorahy, M. J., & van der Hart, O. (2007). Relationship between trauma and dissociation: A historical analysis. In E. Vermetten, M. J. Dorahy, & D. Spiegel (Eds.), *Traumatic dissociation: Neurobiology and treatment* (pp. 3–30). Washington, DC: American Psychiatric Publishing.

Dube, S. R., Anda, R. F., Felitti, V. J., Chapman, D. P., Williamson, D. F., & Giles, W. H. (2001). Childhood abuse, household dysfunction, and the risk of attempted suicide through the life span: Findings from the adverse childhood experiences study. *JAMA, 286*(24), 3089–3096.

Dunbar, R. (1998). The social brain hypothesis. *Evolutionary Anthropology, 6*(5), 178–190.

Eckman, P. (2003). *Emotions revealed.* New York: Henry Holt.

Edwards, V. J., Holden, G. W., Felitti, V. J., & Anda, R. F. (2003). Relationship between multiple forms of childhood maltreatment and adult mental health in community respondents: Results from the adverse childhood experiences study. *American Journal of Psychiatry, 160*(8), 1453–1460.

Fabrega, H. (2002). *Origins of psychopathology: The phylogenetic and cultural basis of mental illness.* New Brunswick, NJ: Rutgers University Press.

Felitti, V. J., Anda, R. F., Nordenberg, D., Williamson, D. F., Spitz, A. M., Edwards, V., Koss, M. P, Marks, J.F. (1998). Relationship of childhood abuse and household dysfunction to many of the leading causes of death in adults. *American Journal of Preventative Medicine, 14,* 245–258.

Foucault, M. (1970). *The order of things: An archaeology of the human sciences.* New York: Random House. (Original work published 1966)

Foucault, M. (1972). *The archaeology of knowledge and the discourse on language* (R. Swyer, Trans.). New York: Pantheon. (Original work published 1971)

Foucault, M. (1988). Technologies of the self. In H. G. Luther, H. Martin, Patrick H. Hutton (Eds.), *Technologies of the self: A seminar with Michel Foucault*. Amherst: University of Massachusetts Press.

Foucault, M. (1990). *The use of pleasure* (R. Hurley, Trans.) (Vol. II). New York: Vantage. (Original work published 1984)

Frazier, P. A., Gavian, M., Perera, S., & Anders, S. (2007, August 17). *Prevalence and effects of traumatic life events among university students*. Paper presented at the American Psychological Association.

Freud, S. (1994). *Civilization and its discontents* (J. Riviere, Trans.). New York: Dover. (Original work published 1930)

Friedman, T. L. (2005). *The world is flat*. New York: Farrar, Straus and Giroux.

Giddens, A. (1994). Living in a post-traditional society. In A. G. Ulrich Beck & Scott Lash (Eds.), *Reflexive modernization: Politics, tradition and aesthetics in the modern social order*. Stanford, CA: Stanford University Press.

Giddens, A. (1999). Reith lectures 1999: Runaway world with Anthony Giddens as lecturer. *Reith Lectures*. Retrieved April 5, 2010 from http://news.bbc.co.uk /hi/english/static/events/reith_99/

Glendinning, C. (1994). *"My name is Chellis & I'm in recovery from Western Civilization."* Boston: Shambhala.

Goodwin, F. K., & Jamison, K. R. (1990). *Manic-depressive illness*. New York: Oxford University Press.

Gottschalk, S. (2000). Escape from insanity: 'Mental disorder' in the postmodern moment. In D. Fee (Ed.), *Pathology and the postmodern: Mental illness as discourse and experience* (pp. 18–48). London: Sage.

Hacking, I. (1991). The making and molding of child abuse. *Critical Inquiry, 17*(Winter), 253–288.

Hacking, I. (1995). *Rewriting the soul: Multiple personality and the sciences of memory.* Princeton, NJ: Princeton University Press.

Hall, W. (Writer). (2009, March 30). Sane medication policy: Robert Whitaker. In W. Hall (Producer), *Madness Radio.* USA: WXOJ-LP FM Radio. Retrieved April 18 from http://www.madnessradio.net/madness-radio-sane-medication-policy-robert-whitaker.

Herman, J. (1997). *Trauma and recovery: The aftermath of violence—from domestic abuse to political terror.* New York: BasicBooks.

Hillman, J. (1972). *The myth of analysis.* Evanston, IL: Northwestern University Press.

Hillman, J. (1975). *Re-visioning psychology.* New York: Harper Perennial.

Hollis, J. (2000). *The archetypal imagination.* College Station, TX: Texas A & M University Press.

Hyde, L. (1998). *Trickster makes this world.* New York: North Point Press.

Jablonka, E., & Lamb, M. J. (2005). *Evolution in four dimensions: Genetic, epigenetic, behavioral, and symbolic variation in the history of life.* Cambridge, MA: The MIT Press.

Jensen, D. (2006). *Endgame: The problem of civilization* (Vol. I). New York: Seven Stories Press.

Jung, C. G. (1933). *Modern man in search of soul* (W. S. Dell & C. F. Baynes, Trans.). New York: Harcourt.

Jung, C. G. (1972). On the psychology of the Trickster figure. In P. Radin (Ed.), *The Trickster: A study in American Indian mythology* (pp. 195–211). New York: Schocken. (Original work published 1956)

Jung, C. G. (1983). On the psychology of the unconscious. In A. Storr (Ed.), *The essential Jung* (pp. 147–167). Princeton, NJ: Princeton University Press. (Original work published 1917/1926/1943)

Jung, C. G. (1983). The undiscovered self (present and future). In A. Storr (Ed.), *The essential Jung* (pp. 349–403). Princeton, NJ: Princeton University Press. (Original work published 1957)

Jung, C. G. (1989). *Memories, dreams, reflections* (A. Jaffé, Ed.) (R. Winston & C. Winston, Trans.). New York: Vintage. (Original work published 1961)

Jung, C. G. (2009). *The red book: Liber novus* (S. Shamdasani, Ed.) (M. Kyburz, J. Peck, & S. Shamdasani, Trans.). New York: W. W. Norton.

Kalsched, D. (1996). *The inner world of trauma: Archetypal defenses of the personal spirit.* New York: Routledge.

Karp, D. A. (1996). *Speaking of sadness*. New York: Oxford University Press.

Kendler, K. S. (2005). "A gene for . . .": The nature of gene action in psychiatric disorders. *American Journal of Psychiatry, 162*(7), 1243–1252.

Kerr, L. K. (2000). *How we become mentally ill* (Doctoral dissertation). Stanford University, Stanford, CA. Available from Proquest database. AAT 9995239.

Kerr, L. K. (2007). Georges Canguilhem and the 'new normal'. In G. Iwele, L. Kerr, & V. Y. Mudimbe (Eds.), *The normal & its orders: Reading Georges Canguilhem* (pp. 152–163). Ottowa: Editions Malaika.

Klein, N. (2007). *The shock doctrine: The rise of disaster capitalism*. New York: Metropolitan.

Kuhn, T. S. (1996). *The structure of scientific revolutions*. Chicago: University of Chicago Press.

Laing, R. D. (1969). *The divided self*. London: Penguin.

Lappé, F. M. (2004, July 14). *Choosing courage in a culture of fear*. Paper presented at Waging peace: Practical approaches to a violent world. Stanford University: Stanford, CA.

Levine, P. (1997). *Waking the tiger: Healing trauma*. Berkeley, CA: North Atlantic Books.

Liedloff, J. (1985). *The continuum concept*. New York: DaCapo Press.

Linden, D. J. (2007). *The accidental mind: How brain evolution has given us love, memory, dreams, and God*. Cambridge, MA: The Belknap Press of Harvard University Press.

Linehan, M. (1993). *Skills training manual for treating borderline personality disorder*. New York: Guilford Press.

Lunbeck, E. (1994). *The psychiatric persuasion: Knowledge, gender, and power in modern America*. Princeton, NJ: Princeton University Press.

Luhrmann, T. M. (2001). *Of two minds: An anthropologist looks at American psychiatry* (2nd ed.). New York: Vintage.

Lyons-Ruth, K., Dutra, L., Schuder, M., & Bianchi, I. (2006). From infant attachment disorganization to adult dissociation: Relational adaptations or traumatic experiences? *Psychiatric Clinics of North America, 29*(1), 63–86.

Maxmen, J. S., Ward, N. G., & Kilgus, M. (2009). *Essential psychopathology & its treatment* (3rd ed.). New York: W. W. Norton.

McFarlane, A. C., & Kolk, B. A. v. d. (1996). Trauma and its challenge to society. In B. A. van der Kolk, A. C. McFarlane & L. Weisaeth (Eds.), *Traumatic stress: The effects of overwhelming experience on mind, body, and society* (pp. 24–46). New York: The Guilford Press.

McNally, R. J. (2003). *Remembering trauma*. Cambridge, MA: The Belknap Press.

Moore, T. (2008). *A life at work: The joy of discovering what you were born to do*. New York: Broadway.

Mulhern, S. (1991). Embodied alternative identities: Bearing witness to a world that might have been. *Psychiatric Clinics of North America, 14*(3), 769–787.

Mythen, G. (2004). *Ulrich Beck: A critical introduction to risk society*. London: Pluto Press.

Nash, J. M. (2007, January 29). The gift of mimicry. *Time,* 108–113.

Nussbaum, M. (2006, September 13). *Equal liberty of conscience: Roger Williams and the roots of a constitutional tradition*. Paper presented at the Foerster Lectures, University of California, Berkeley.

Ogawa, J., Sroufe, L. A., Weinfield, N. S., Carlson, E., & Egeland, B. (1997). Development and the fragmented self: A longitudinal study of dissociative symptomatology in a non-clinical sample. *Developmental Psychopathology, 4*, 855–879.

Oxford English dictionary. (1989). (2nd ed.). Oxford, UK: Oxford University Press.

Pelton, R. (1989). *The Trickster in West Africa*. Los Angeles: University of California Press.

Putnam, F. W. (1997). *Dissociation in children and adolescents*. New York: Guilford Press.

Rabinow, P. (Ed.). (1994). *Michel Foucault: Ethics, subjectivity, and truth, volume I*. New York: The New Press.

Radin, P. (1972). *The Trickster: A study in American Indian mythology*. New York: Schocken Books.

Ramachandran, V. S., & Oberman, L. M. (2006, November). Broken mirrors: A theory of autism. *Scientific American,* 63–69.

Risch, N., Herrell, R., Lehner, T., Liang, K. Y., Eaves, L., Hoh, J., Griem, A., Kovacs, M., Ott, J., Rie Merikangas, K. (2009).

Interaction between the serotonin transporter gene (5-HTTLPR), stressful life events, and risk of depression: A meta-analysis. *JAMA, 301*(23), 2462–2471.

Rizzolatti, G., & Craighero, L. (2004). The mirror-neuron system. *Annual Review of Neuroscience, 27,* 169–192.

Rizzolatti, G., Fogassi, L., & Gallese, V. (2006, November). Mirrors in the mind. *Scientific American,* 54–61.

Romanyshyn, R. D. (2007). *The wounded researcher.* New Orleans: Spring Journal Books.

Samuels, A. (1985). Archetypal psychology. In *Jung and the post-Jungians* (pp. 241–248). London, UK: Routledge.

Sapolsky, R. (2005). Sick of poverty. *Scientific American,* 93–99.

Schmitt, E. (2001, May 15). For the first time, nuclear families drop below 25% of households. *New York Times.*

Shapiro, F. (2001). *Eye movement desensitization and reprocessing (EMDR): Basic principles, protocols, and procedures* (2nd ed.). New York: The Guilford Press.

Shenk, D. (1997). *Data smog: Surviving the information glut.* New York: HarperEdge.

Shepard, P. (1982). *Nature and madness*. Athens: University of Georgia Press.

Singh-Manoux, A., Adler, N. E., & Marmot, M. G. (2003). Subjective social status: Its determinants and its association with measures of ill-health in the Whitehall II study. *Social Science & Medicine, 56*, 1321–1333.

Steinberg, M., & Schnall, M. (2000). *The stranger in the mirror: Dissociation—the hidden epidemic*. New York: HarperCollins.

Szasz, T. (2001). *Pharmacracy: Medicine and politics in America*. Westport, CT: Praeger.

Tomich, P. (2007, August 17). *Different traumatic life events: Different amounts of distress or growth?* Paper presented at the American Psychological Association, San Francisco, California.

Turner, E. H., Matthews, A. M., Linardatos, E., Tell, R. A., & Rosenthal, R. (2008). Selective publication of antidepressant trials and its influence on apparent efficacy. *New England Journal of Medicine, 358*, 252–260.

Turner, J. H. (2000). *On the origins of human emotions*. Stanford, CA: Stanford University Press.

Van der Kolk, B. (2008, January 14). *The neurobiology of complex trauma*. Paper presented at the National Child Traumatic Stress Network Training Seminar. Retrieved on January 14, 2008, from http://www.nctsnet.org/.

Van der Kolk, B., McFarlane, A. C., & Weisaeth, L. (Eds.). (1996). *Traumatic stress: The effects of overwhelming experience on mind, body, and society*. New York: The Guilford Press.

Van der Kolk, B. A., Weisaeth, L., & van der Hart, O. (1996). History of trauma in psychiatry. In B. A. van der Kolk, A. C. McFarlane, & L. Weisaeth (Eds.), *Traumatic stress: The effects of overwhelming experience on mind, body, and society* (pp. 47–74). New York: The Guilford Press.

Van der Post, L. (1961). *The heart of the hunter*. New York: William Morrow.

Whitfield, C. L. (2004). *The truth about mental illness: Choices for healing*. Deerfield Beach, FL: Health Communications.

Wicker, B., Keysers, C., Plailly, J., Royet, J.-P., Gallese, V., & Rizzolatti, G. (2003). Both of us disgusted in my insula: The common neural basis of seeing and feeling disgust. *Neuron, 40,* 655–664.

Wilkerson, A. L. (1998). "Her body her own worst enemy": The medicalization of violence against women. In S. G. French, W. Teays, & L. M. Purdy (Eds.), *Violence against women: Philosophical perspectives* (pp. 123–138). Ithaca, NY: Cornell University Press.

Wilkinson, M. (2006). *Coming into mind*. New York: Routledge.

ABOUT THE AUTHOR

Laura K. Kerr, PhD is a scholar and former psychotherapist specialized in sensorimotor psychotherapy. Though her primary focus is trauma and its effects, her interests are varied, with degrees in physics, atmospheric and space science, philosophy, counseling psychology, and the philosophy of education and symbolic systems.

Dr. Kerr has published numerous articles, book chapters, encyclopedia entries, and a collection of essays, *Trauma's Labyrinth: Reflections of a Wounded Healer*. She is currently at work on her next two books: one on the evolution of spirituality and the other on recovery from sexual trauma.

She lives in San Francisco, CA with her husband. When not writing nonfiction, she gardens, paints, writes poetry, practices yoga, and enjoys nature. Visit her at laurakkerr.com.

www.ingramcontent.com/pod-product-compliance
Lightning Source LLC
Chambersburg PA
CBHW070123030426
42335CB00016B/2254